Angel of Disruption

Angel of Disruption

THE GRIM UNDERSIDE OF A REAL-LIFE FAIRY TALE

Mara Kendahl

Parker Street Books

Parker Street Books
Published by Parker Street Books
Newark, NJ 07104

First Parker Street Books Printing, May 2017

Copyright © Mara Kendahl, 2017
All rights reserved.

ISBN: 0999029304
ISBN 13: 9780999029305

Cover photograph is from the author's collection.

for Wallace Berger, her father, and her brothers

Contents

Author's Note · xiii

Fairy Tale Part 1: Orphan · 1

More Than Potatoes · 3

Last Stop · 9

Hushed · 13

Fairy Tale Part 2: Quest · 15

Travelogue First Trip: Moscow · 17

This Place Sucks · 20

Travelogue First Trip: Komsomolsk-Na-Amur · · · · · · · · · · 23

I'm All That · 30

Travelogue First Trip: Problem ·32

Help! ·35

Travelogue First Trip: Khabarovsk ·39

The Bus Ride Back ·41

Travelogue First Trip: Baby House #2 · · · · · · · · · · · · · · · · · ·44

Found Him ·45

Perfect ·48

Travelogue Second Trip: Return to Baby House #2 · · · · · · ·55

Kangaroo Court ·60

Travelogue Second Trip: Almost Home · · · · · · · · · · · · · · · · ·63

Black and Proud ·66

Natalia's Bibles ·71

Fairy Tale Part 3: Damaged · 73

Hey, Blogosphere! ·75

Jungle Gym Fun ·79

Notes for the DDD · 82

Everyone's A Hammer · 90

48 Out of 50 · 93

Fairy Tale Part 4: Chaos · 101

Stealing · 103

Hundred Dollar School Day · 105

Sheets To The Wind · 110

Itchy · 115

County Team · 118

No More Running Around · 120

In Pencil · 122

Dear Parents · 125

Chapter 5 A Fairy Tale: Disruption · · · · · · · · · · · · · · 127

Try Something New · 129

Show Me The Money · 133

Summers ·136

Baby Cousin ·140

It Really Could Have ·143

Stolen ·145

Blood Oranges ·147

Making Everyone Crazy ·158

Stomach Ache ·162

What'd I Miss ·166

Black Eye Bags ·168

False ·171

Hazel's Concert ·176

More Eye Bags ·179

Fairy Tale Part 6: Miracle · 183

Why ·185

A Wild West Inquiry ·190

Paradigm	191
Recurring Drama	194
Intercession	200
Welcome to the Ranch	202
Keep It Clean	203
Ask	205
And Ye Shall Receive	207
Sources	211

Author's Note

As a child, I feared a legal kidnapping. I worried that strangers would show up at the front door and claim me, take me away from my home, family, and friends. Any adopted kid will understand this concern. It wasn't a constant worry, though. The occasional realization that it *could* happen was a fleeting, recurring irritation throughout childhood.

By the time I was a teen, I rarely acknowledged my status as an adopted child. I'd be reminded every so often, though, in doctor's offices. They'd advise me to stay out of the sun, because my mom had a history of skin cancer. My mom and I would nod, and I'd run home to tan.

As an adult, I realized how fortunate I was to have been adopted by wonderful parents. I was not their adopted daughter; I was their daughter, period. There could have been no better family than mine.

Once I was married and had my own family, I started to give more thought to adoption. I felt called to "pay it forward." My unsuspecting husband was shocked when I told him my intention. We had been together over seven years, and I had never mentioned it. Good man that he is, he supported me.

The story you are about to read is true, except for the details in Part 1 which are invented based on information provided at the orphanage. I've taken pains to change the names of all private individuals involved, including my own. Some persons and business entities have received public attention in the mainstream media and may be recognizable. I've provided a few citations at the end of this book if you care to investigate.

All events are depicted based on my own memory. I've tried to keep all events, correspondence, and conversations as accurate as possible. The responsibility for any inaccuracies is mine. My apologies in advance for any errors or omissions; it was a chaotic time.

The experiences in this book are uniquely mine, yet countless families experience similar situations. Health, education, and government services are judgmental and unhelpful. There's little understanding, scant assistance, and no respite to be found. The incredible toll, the sacrifice, the loneliness, the desperation is unfathomable to those who don't know first-hand the struggle of raising a disabled child. My family's journey and ultimate decision was harrowing, but in the best interest of all involved. That didn't make our choices any easier.

I hope this book can make you, just one reader, one parent, feel encouraged and supported amid the chaos that has become your new "normal." You are a good parent; you are trying your best; you are doing what's right; you are not alone. Someone should tell you that. Let it be me.

Fairy Tale Part 1: Orphan

Once upon a time there was a boy named--what was his name? He lived with his mommy who was very poor. His mommy couldn't keep him safe and healthy because she wasn't safe and healthy herself, so while he was still a tiny baby, she left him with strangers and never returned. Those strangers couldn't keep him, though. They turned him over to the police, and he became an orphan. He went to an orphanage, a mean, ugly place where he grew frail and scabby waiting with the other little orphans for a family.

More Than Potatoes

Anya stared out the cracked window from her kitchen chair. From the gray 5th floor apartment, there was nothing to see but the frozen road below and the snow covered plains beyond. Her father, on the couch, snored and coughed while the pipes in the walls whined. This housing block on the outskirts of Khabarovsk was in grave disrepair, always moaning and clanking. It was true Soviet style: a cement box unfinished outside with no hint of plaster, paint, or embellishment. No niceties dared adorn this homely structure punctuated with metal windowless doors, one lurching crookedly on its hinges. Snow piled high against one side, covering the first and second story windows until late spring. Inside, grungy ivory lead paint clung to the cement walls of Anya's kitchen. The smell of boiled cabbage and her father's stale breath permeated even the cement.

The electricity was working that day, so Anya watched the state run television channel on the small black-and-white on the kitchen counter. Happy women in clean, new clothing wearing healthy complexions, straight teeth, and heeled shoes smiled out at her. She smiled her crooked smile and looked down at her boots.

Mother had told her she was a good girl, and that good girls would marry well and be rewarded with a tidy home and warm food. So far, she had few hopes of marrying, tidiness, or abundant meals. And Mother wasn't around to help. Her cough had progressed, and one dim morning Anya awoke to find her cold. Mother's state pension was revoked at her death, leaving the family with only Father's pension, which he drank most of, leaving Anya scrounging for bread and soup. She dreamed of meat and cheese and wine. Instead, broth, black bread and vodka most days. The meager harvest of beets and potatoes from the buckets she tended carefully by the kitchen window was welcome indeed.

She opened the front door to check for the grubby sack that she hoped would be sitting there. It was. Dirty laundry dropped off by the ancient widower down the hall. "It's money" she told herself as she tied back her blond hair and bent over the sink.

At the market waiting for the daily bread delivery later that bitter morning, Anya noticed her schoolmate, Varvara, a plain girl with crooked teeth and a creepy older brother whom most girls avoided. Once, they had been friends, sharing homework and giggles. Varvara left school last year, and Anya hadn't seen her since. Today, Varvara looked sophisticated, her one front tooth crossed partway over the other elegantly instead of snaggly as Anya remembered. Varvara stood confidently on line in her new coat and fur cap. Anya admired her former schoolmate and called to her impulsively.

"*Dobre Utra*, Varvara! How are you, sister?"

"Well, Anya, I'm doing well. How's your father?" she replied.

"Alive. You look lovely, Varvara. Have you married?"

"No, have you?" She eyed Anya, and knew she hadn't.

"Ha!," Anya snorted. "But Varvara, you look so well."

"Don't I, Anya? I have a job in the city at the Khabarovsk Intourist Hotel. Have you heard of it? I get to meet new people and buy new clothes and live a little."

"Oh, I'm happy for you," Anya lied. Her downcast face alerted Varvara to the lie.

"Don't be jealous, Anyushka. Is it so bad?"

Anya told Varvara of her troubles, of her desire to see more than the view from her kitchen window, to eat more than her paltry potato crop from the buckets by the window. She turned her flushed face away and wiped a budding tear with her laundry-chapped hands.

Varvara said, "Anya, there might be work for you, too. I'll ask my brother Kirill if he can use you. He's the boss."

Anya squeaked out her thanks though her tightened throat. Work! When Varvara got her bread ration and hurried away with a wave and a smile, Anya suppressed the urge to run after her. Instead, she stood rooted to the cold ground, powdery snow swirling in small circles about her feet like dreams that didn't dare rise higher.

Varvara was true to her word. Three days later, Anya accepted the bus fare Kirill sent and listened to her own heartbeat in her temples as she bumped along on the evening local to Khabarovsk. She sat among the dusty laborers and weary factory workers and fiddled with broken threads on the tattered strap of her vinyl pocketbook. The bus stopped every few blocks for the tired to shuffle on and off, clutching their worn coats and bags. Sparse cinder block housing gave way to small houses and then larger cinderblock apartments. Soon, there were grand buildings with stolid and stark facades, imposing Soviet statues of workers–men and women with broad faces and strong hands–along Muravyov-Amursky street. Work would make her strong and proud like the silent statues, she hoped.

As planned, Kirill was waiting for her beneath the statue of Captain Jacob Dyachenko at the side of the Intourist Hotel. The Captain's dead, stony face surveyed the square, judging, his hand on one hip and cloak forever thrown back. Kirill, looking less powerful but just as haughty, waved to her from the base of the statue. Even sporting a crisp new black jacket with buckles at the neck and waist, and what seemed to be American blue jeans, Kirill was not handsome. A layer of grime seemed to cover him, his too shiny hair, his tobacco stained teeth. He greeted her with a kiss as though they were old friends, and slid his arm around her waist. She suffered his touch and his sour breath as he led her around the back entrance of the hotel and down to the basement lounge.

The mirrored room was awash in light, music, and laughter. Lovely young women cozied up to well-dressed middle-aged men. As Kirill guided Anya among them, she noticed the women weren't pretty close up, the Russian men were overdressed and sloppy, and the foreigners were as soft as children. Varvara wasn't there, though Anya craned her neck hoping to spot her.

Kirill acted the big shot with the girls, waving at this one, pointing and winking slyly at that one. He sat Anya at the bar and signaled to the bartender, who ambled over with a weary look of pity and placed a cold vodka shot on the sticky bar in front of Anya. Kirill gestured for her to drink.

"The bar area is where you'll be stationed." he cooed, keeping his arm around her waist. Anya asked about the rooms she would be cleaning.

Kirill snorted. "Just make yourself pleasant. Have another drink. You are here to entertain. Be entertaining."

She knew. While Kirill motioned again to the barman, she admitted to herself that she had known all along. He left her staring straight ahead, and she downed the next ice cold vodka the barman served.

Kirill returned with a paunchy older Russian from St. Petersburg whom he introduced as an old friend and settled in the seat next to Anya's. After some niceties, the man held forth about his troubles at his manufacturing business, some sort of paper bag factory. But she wasn't listening. Instead she asked the bartender for another, and then just one more. She offered a nervous smile to the man from St. Petersburg who eventually put his moist, beefy hand on her thigh. Soon after, the man made a quick sign, like a customer signaling a waiter, and Kirill appeared. The two men whispered, and Kirill pressed a key into the man from St. Petersburg's meaty hand. The man stood and stretched. Anya smelled Kirill's sweat and aftershave when he leaned his face too close to hers and pressed his hand on her lower back.

"Anya, you go with this man. You will be paid well for your time. Go now, don't embarrass me."

Yes, she had known all along. So why hesitate? She'd been kidding herself since she ran into Varvara that cold morning.

She knew. Of course she knew. She heard herself chuckle dryly and noticed that many of the girls who'd been in the bar earlier were now gone. Some older women were chortling with sad looking foreigners at a corner table overflowing with glasses. *You will be paid well for your time*, Kirill had said.

"My time," she said out loud to no one, as the businessman led her by the hand to the elevator. She'd return home with money in that hand, she thought. Father will be pleased when he wakes up. *What would Mama think?* she wondered. Kirill's "Don't embarrass me" echoed in her vodka soaked thoughts. Mama is dead. The corners of her mouth sagged, and gooseflesh dotted her arms. At the door to room 326, while the man from St. Petersburg fumbled with the key, Anya strained to focus on the scruffy stray hairs on the back of his neck, hairs that should have been shaved clean.

From the window of room 326 in the Intourist Hotel she could see the Amur river snaking and turning and leading far away.

Later, Kirill stuffed a handful of rubles and a bus ticket into her tired vinyl purse. He kissed her roughly on her mouth and smirked, "Come back tomorrow night?" They both knew she'd be back.

Last Stop

The view of the snowy road below is starting to blur again. A welcome deliverance. Weak cries reach her rickety kitchen chair by the window; the baby's whining again. Tiny cries, not healthy nor hearty, but soft and steady, the kind that don't seem urgent. But they are. She knows he's putting his whole soul into emitting this small whimper. It's all he's got. Weak, small, he's dwindling, just like Father. His round baby's head is larger than his sinewy, dried out body. Small hands clutch at the air, at the future, at nothing. She wobbles to the sofa and finds him where she remembers leaving him, asleep in the crook of Father's arm. Father's sleeping, too, and the infant's frail squirming isn't enough to wake him. When was the last time she'd fed either of them? There's not enough food anymore.

Kirill had sneered and sent her home once she started to show. No more work, and her government check will continue for only one more month. *What a crime that they pay stipend for only 6 months following childbirth. It should be a year*, Anya concludes. How will she care for the baby without money? Who will watch him when she returns to work? *Father? Ha! They will both die*. After another drink, she chews her bottom lip and wonders if that wouldn't be a good thing.

Anya sips the morning away, contemplating. *My life–this is it? Caring for this drunken Father and this limp infant?*

After a lunch of boiled potatoes and vodka for her, mashed beets for baby, and nothing for Father who won't wake up, she deposits the baby once again in the crook of Father's arm and goes to bed herself. She dreams of Mother, for the first time in years.

In the dream, Anya is sitting in her usual place by the window and sees Mother walking on the snow-covered road below, coughing and clutching at the neck of her ragged coat. At first, Mother doesn't see her, and she fears Mother may disappear without noticing her. She wants to call out, but she takes a drink instead. She looks deep into the drained cup, then back out the window to find Mother staring at her, into her eyes. Neither looks away. Suddenly, Mother's face contorts into a wail, a long, silent scream. Anya struggles to open the window, but it disintegrates in her hands at her touch, letting the cold in, filling the apartment with swirling snow that gathers around her feet in drifts.

Then, Mother is standing in the kitchen, amidst the drifts, still clutching her coat, still staring, but now stone faced. Close up, Mother smells like dirt. In the dream, Anya wonders why Mother is standing there. She thought Mother had died cold in her bed from a cough that lodged in her throat, then her chest, then her soul. *Mother, aren't you dead?* Mother reaches out a familiar hand and caresses Anya's cheek. *Oh, you're back now, right, Mother?*

Mother seems to hear Anya's thoughts and shakes her head, still staring into Anya's uncertain face. *Now*, Mother's mouth forms the word soundlessly, and again, *Now, Now!*, until all Anya can see is Mother's silent, moving lips, forming the word over and over in eery silence.

Anya wakes up startled and parched. She shuffles to prepare tea and takes it at her seat by the window, but she doesn't look out. She can't shake the dream away.

The child is stirring; Father is silent. Father feels cool when she picks up the boy to change him. Her hand to Father's forehead. Colder. Her hand to his neck. Too cold, too still.

• • •

In the thin days following Father's death, Anya often finds herself staring out the window or at the child. She's decided.

She dresses for work on Thursday afternoon and takes one drink. Although she'd promised herself earlier that she wouldn't drink today, she cannot abide. Preparing the baby for the weather, she realizes he looks almost healthy wrapped in his yellow blanket, his too-thin limbs hidden in the blanket's bulk.

On the bus, the baby boy doesn't cry nor sleep; he looks around, alert. *He knows*, she thinks. The bus ride to the Intourist Hotel is much longer than she remembers. The Intourist stop comes and goes, and Anya and the boy sit in silence on the noisy bus as laden passengers lumber on and off. No one notices the young woman and her son as they ride through the center of town and up, out, toward the northern edge of the town's outskirts. Anya clutches the neck of her coat and exits at the last stop, near a cement apartment building sprouting out of the snow like a poison mushroom, much like her own, now over an hour away.

It is best, she prods herself. She remains at the bus stop, waiting. Two old women approach, bickering. Anya rushes towards them, meeting them before they reach the bus stop.

"Ladies, I'm lost!," she cries.

Their diffidence softens as they eye the yellow bundle.

"I was supposed to meet my cousin, but I must have taken the wrong bus!"

Confused and vague conversation ensues regarding where she was going, where she went, and how to return. Small beads of moisture are forming on Anya's brow, but the women don't notice. The boy stirs frailly. *Now*, thought Anya. *Now*.

"Dear Ladies, will you please watch my boy for just a moment while I go buy some milk? We've been on the bus so long, and he is hungry. It's too cold to keep him outside. Won't you please? I'll be right back!" Her eyes implored, and she was right; it was cold. She felt the chill on the moisture surfacing on her upper lip. A quick swipe of her hand removed it.

A strange request, but the girl is strange. And lost. What harm in tending the child a moment? A beautiful child. They agree. They will take the boy inside to warm him, and she will return right away with milk.

"*Dosvedanya, Dima*," she whispers, pressing a quick kiss on his cheek before handing him to outstretched arms.

Hushed

In the dim nighttime lobby of the grey building just beyond the bus route's last stop, there's an unlikely gathering. Two old, scarf-wrapped women, two decrepit, fur capped men, two uniformed officers, and one swaddled baby congregate in quiet discussion: various brows lowered, mouths downturned, hands gesturing, aged shoulders hunched against the chill. Curled awkwardly in the arms of the younger officer, the baby contributes a spattering of cries. Questions, explanations. More questions. Explanations run thin. Presently, the officers drive away with the baby, and the old men and women remain, theorizing, hushed, gossiping awhile before retreating to their bleak apartments to conjecture.

Fairy Tale Part 2: ~~Quest~~

*S*oon, a new mommy came from far, far away. She named the little orphan boy Ricky and wanted to take him home with her. But the orphanage was like a prison, with strict rules and evil workers who made it hard to get him out. After a long struggle, the wicked people let baby Ricky go home to a happy new family.

Travelogue First Trip: Moscow

~~~Friday, January 24th, Newark, NJ, 4:30 p.m.~~~

Dear Bert, Alex, and Hazel,

You guys just dropped me off at Newark airport. You asked me to keep a log for you all, so I'm starting right away. Bert, you seem nervous for me. Alex, you know what's going on; you're concerned that I shouldn't forget to bring you a present. Hazel, you held your arms up for a kiss and were on the verge of tears. You said, "I'm going to MISS you, Mommy!" Leaving you with that look on your little face and your pretty curls flying everywhere made me want to cry, but I didn't have time. They started getting me through the security line–I even had to take my shoes off. I'll be sure to wear these ugly slip-on shoes I just bought for the rest of the flights.

So guys, I'm on my way to Russia to look at this "new boy" of ours. I'm a little nervous. What will he be like? He didn't look so healthy on the new video we got yesterday. I hope he's ok. I'm still sitting here waiting in Newark for the Frankfurt flight to board.

~~~Tuesday, Komsomolsk-na-Amur, 3:30 a.m.~~~

Hi again, guys. It's been a few days since I wrote. I'm sitting in an almost comfortable hotel room in Komsomolsk-na-Amur, a 6-hour bus ride from Khabarovsk. I'm at a little dining table having a cheese sandwich I saved from earlier and a cup of tea. Let me try to pick up where I left off. So much has happened.

The 4 ½ hour ride from Frankfurt to Moscow was tedious, because I couldn't sleep. Oh, and the flight from Newark to Frankfurt was about 7 hours 45 minutes. I slept a little on the first flight. Both flights were long and boring, but thankfully smooth and uneventful.

When I arrived in Moscow, there was a pretty brown-haired woman my age holding a sign with my name on it. She introduced herself as Angela, and we went right away to exchange $1,500 and to buy my airplane ticket to Khabarovsk. Then we went outside to a car and driver waiting for us, and she explained that my destination was not Khabarovsk, as I had thought, but Komsomolsk-na-Amur, 6 hours away from Khabarovsk. I wasn't happy. I asked why they'd move an orphan boy 6 hours away, and no one could answer the question. They took me to the Ukraina Hotel, where they quickly left me. My impression was that Angela was in a big hurry. I had asked to go sightseeing, but she was not free the following day. (It was already dinner time by the time I got to the hotel.) When I insisted, she said she would find someone to take me out.

So there I was in Moscow alone, around 8:00 p.m. Moscow time, in a dark crummy little room, not knowing what on earth to do with myself. No tv, no radio, and the bed was sunken in a whole foot lower in the middle than on the sides. I wasn't too sleepy, so I went to call you guys in the "business center" on the second floor. The hotel staff were serious, stern and unfriendly, even the young people. When I got to the business center, I couldn't get a line out to call home, and when I did it would drop after saying a few words. I'm glad you could hear me when I kept repeating "email" over the bad phone connection. Then it cost me 75 roubles to use the internet for 10 minutes to send you that email to say I was okay.

This Place Sucks

———— Original Message ————

From: Margot
To: Bert
Subject: This place sucks

Dear Bert,

This place is the worst, and everything seems to be going wrong already. The flight was long, the agents that met me were rude and confusing, and now I've been dumped here with no food until tomorrow. Cranky? You bet.

    Joseph called the hotel earlier to check in on me. Remember I told you about him? I know you said you didn't want to be bothered with the minutia, but you should at least know who our representatives are and why.

    Joseph's the guy who ran the first adoption agency we contracted, and then his agency got shut down after we paid our money but before we could get to Russia. I never really gave you the scoop on him. They closed him because someone reported that he was involved in child porn while he was in college. The truth of the matter, as Joseph tells it, was that he worked as a freelance web designer to pay his way through college. (I love the guy–a real go-getter.) Anyway, he didn't discriminate. If you were a paying customer, he designed your website, no judgement. Well, he should have discriminated. When the state got wind of it they confiscated all his files, ours included, and locked them in a vault in Cherry Hill and said our case was closed. That was when I got hold of that reporter and the whole story hit the Star-Ledger (I know you remember that part!), and then that horrible woman from Trenton grudgingly gave us all our files back. That's why we're with Tanya now. She took on many of Joseph's cases. So even though we have to work with Tanya, who I'm not so fond of, it was Joseph who called to check in on me. The guy is in a world of trouble and *he's* checking on *me*. God bless him.

Anyway, I was feeling tired, unwelcome, and hungry in that ugly little room upstairs before, and I was probably whine-y and complain-y to Joseph (and I regret it). I asked him to call you to tell you all's well. I know you were worried when I called, and all I could hear was your voice distorted over the line like in the movies when kidnappers don't want their voices detected. I'm sorry! I hope you weren't hearing the same thing! I could tell the connection was bad, but there was nothing I could do. The phone lines here are primitive.

I asked Joseph to contact Tanya and tell her to call me, and about an hour later she did. I complained about the interpreter ditching me and the unexplained change of destination.

Mara Kendahl

So for the record, my destination is no longer Khabarovsk, but Komsomolsk-na-Amur. I don't even know where that is, and the internet is too slow here. I don't have the patience to wait for the photos to download. If you get this email, please look the place up and tell me where the heck I'm going.

Love and miss you,
Margot

Travelogue First Trip: Komsomolsk-Na-Amur

So guys, in the business center while I was trying to get the stupid computer to work, I met a woman in her 40's who had waited a year for her court date to finalize her adoption. A year. She was travelling with her father on a one-trip adoption in the city of Moscow. Her girl is 5. Moscow is the only city in the country that lets you meet your child and finalize the adoption on the same trip. Everywhere else, you come to meet the child and sign request papers. Then, a judge orders you back for a court date to finalize the adoption a few months later. Moscow takes longer for your paperwork to clear, but at least you only have to travel to Russia once.

I read for an hour in my awful hammock shaped bed. I'm reading "Memoirs of a Geisha" that my friend, Michele from work, gave me. At about 11:30 Moscow time I decide to go to sleep, but the phone rang. A girl named Maria said she'd pick me up at 11 the next morning to go sightseeing for 3 hours. I was thrilled. Cost was $10/hour for both her and the driver, $60 total. That's a lot of rubles. Anyway, I went to sleep tired, thinking I'd sleep around 7-8 hours, and wake up at 6 or 7 am Moscow time. What really happened is I fell asleep for 2 ½ hours and woke up raring to go at 2 in the morning. I must have slept more on the planes than I thought, or the bed was plain uncomfortable, or I'm just good on little sleep thanks to you, Hazel. So I read until about 6 and then dozed on and off for a while. I went downstairs for the hotel's breakfast at what I thought was 9:30, but I miscalculated. It was 10:30, breakfast was over, and Maria would arrive in ½ hour. Darn it.

Maria was waiting in the lobby for me. I had worked up a sweat rushing, because they keep the inside of of buildings dreadfully hot. I don't know why it's so hot everywhere. Tall, blonde Maria was a gorgeous, 24-year-old newlywed who had once been an exchange student in Ohio. She said she could not locate an available driver, so her handsome husband, Nicolai, who spoke no English, would drive us. Together, the two looked like movie stars. (Throughout the day I noticed many strikingly beautiful Russian men and women. Their faces were exquisite, but their attitudes were serious and cranky.)

First Maria and Nicolai took me to Christ Church, a brand new cathedral in town. It was bright and big and packed. Then for pizza at a Sbarro's in a mall. Disappointing. I could have found a Sbarro's myself. Not what I had hoped, but Maria was a kid, and probably thought I'd like pizza. A little local color would have been better.

The Sbarro's cashier made motion for me to pay, and I paid the bill unaware that I paid for all three of us. So cheap! Unfortunately, when Nicolai realized I paid for their meals, he got upset. Maria said her husband felt embarrassed that I paid. Jeez. Instead of just saying thank you, or paying me for his share, he got all sulky about it, and Maria had to soothe him while we ate. Awkward.

Then we went to the Kremlin's Armory Exhibit where they displayed all the czars' costumes, crowns, carriages, and old army equipment from the 1400's to 1700's. It was great. Sometimes school kids would stop and stare at us speaking English. Not peek or glance, but flat out stand right in front of us and plainly stare like they were watching TV. It was funny to me, but it made Maria angry, and sometimes she'd yell at the kids. Short tempers on these folks.

After the Kremlin, we took a brisk walk to Red Square, where we saw Lenin's tomb and St. Basil's cathedral. That's the big cathedral with the colorful pointy mushroom-looking things on top. But we didn't go in because time was short. It was 2:00 already. Angela was picking me up at 3:15 to go to the airport to fly to Khabarovsk.

Angela was right on time. We rode to the airport, and I was telling her about how ugly and frustrating it is to work with her employer, Amrex, the Russian-American agency in charge of adoptions. According to Tanya, they are responsible for all the delays we've had with our paperwork and trip. Angela said it only takes 2-3 weeks to get a court date once the judge has your papers, but that her bosses had told her to never discuss the waiting period with Americans. Maybe because the actual waiting period is 4-5 months. Hmmm. We had tea and a sandwich at the airport before she directed me to my departure gate. She turned out to be quite nice, and I don't think she was happy with her employer either, but at 32 and with an 8-year-old, she needed the job. We arranged for her to take me shopping on my way back through Moscow.

At the gate, I saw a couple that was so obviously American that I went over and introduced myself. John and Mary May from — maybe suburban Chicago? — I already forget. They were friendly, on their second adoption trip to get a 1 ½ year old girl, to have the court date and final adoption, not the first trip just to meet the child and sign papers, like me. Shortly after, we were joined by another American couple the Mays had met in their Moscow hotel, Robert and Diane Barton from Michigan. The Bartons had 2 adopted Russian boys already, had one "bio" boy (that's slang in the "adoption community" for children you had yourself, so Alex and Hazel are "bio" kids!) and were on their second trip to get a 2-year-old girl. I suspect they are Mormons. Anyway, we were laughing and joking and having a grand old time like old friends. All the Russians around us were serious and silent; it was quite a contrast. By luck, I ended up sitting with Robert and Diane on the plane, which was ancient and made lots of terrible scary noises. We chatted and laughed about the sounds and our strange fellow passengers and made the flight fun. After a while, Robert pulled out a whole bottle of Nyquil, took a swig, and said goodnight. Diane took a swig and passed it to me. Why not, it's a 10-hour ride? Slept like a baby until we landed.

The Khabarovsk airport is like out of a Russian movie about communism. The building is a grey block in the middle of miles of nothing but snow. They let us out of the plane on the runway, and we walked 100 yards across the icy runway to the building. We were laughing thinking of all the lawsuits there'd be in the US with people slipping and sliding on the ice and falling on their faces with their carry-on bags. I guess if you fall here, you're on your own. It was so cold it burned my nostrils to breathe. I don't know if that makes sense, but that's how it was.

Inside, I had to part with the Bartons. Natasha (interpreter), Luba (agent), and Sergei (driver) met me and whisked me away. (Can't they just hire an agent who speaks English and drives? Why am I paying three people?) Luba is around 50 and speaks no English at all. Natasha and Sergei are both young and gorgeous. Natasha says I'm lucky to arrive on such a beautiful warm day, it had been cold recently. I thought maybe she was joking, but she wasn't. Why would anyone live here? It's like some frozen, desolate planet too far from the sun.

They dropped me at a hotel to relax and wash up. The twin bed took up the entire room. I stopped at the ratty little desk and ancient computer they call a "business center" and sent you that email about the funny guy on the plane.

Later I bumped into Natasha on the stairs. I was scouring the place for food to no avail. I hadn't had a decent meal since I-don't-know-when. I was so jet lagged and hungry I wasn't sure what day it was. We went to the little hotel cafe, and I had potato dumplings with butter. They were like pierogies. What a relief to eat. (I bought a cheese sandwich and stowed it in my bag, because these people don't give me enough opportunities to eat. It's not like at home where you can just stop at a convenience store. There's nothing for sale anywhere and there's nothing convenient.)

Mara Kendahl

We caught the 2:00 bus to Komsomolsk-na-Amur. Only Luba, who spoke no English at all, rode with me. I slept in my chair until the bus stopped at a small bar in the middle of frozen nowhere, so we could get off and use the bathroom. (There were only about 5 other people on the bus. How does the bus company make money?) After that, I laid down across all the seats in the back of the bus and tried to sleep, but the bus jumped and lurched like an off-road Jeep. As far as I could see, there was only snow and forests of thin black and white trees (birch?) for miles in every direction, and an occasional army-looking truck parked or abandoned, I don't know which, by the side of the road.

When we arrived, Andrei, another handsome young driver, was waiting for us. No interpreter. They left me here at this hotel, where I'm sitting now, and I'm not quite sure what's going on. The hotel is old and broken on the outside. It's so perfectly tumble-down, it looks like Hollywood's version of a ramshackle building, so I was afraid it would be another dump. Instead, it's not bad. The hostess is almost friendly, and she gave me a thermos of hot water to bring to my room for tea. I'm on the second floor, up a wooden spiral staircase. When you walk in, you enter a spacious dining-room/living room area. The bedroom, too, is large with a comfortable double bed. The bathroom is large and clean but antiquated, with a string to pull to flush the toilet. I washed socks and underclothes in the sink and went to sleep. It was probably around 9:00 p.m. here. When I woke up about an hour ago, it was 3 a.m. The TV works, but they don't broadcast anything at this hour. How crazy it that? The things I had washed were dry. Glad I saved that cheese sandwich, so I could have it with this tea.

Pick up time is 9:00 a.m. to go to the orphanage, or at least that's what I think Luba meant when she wrote 9:00 on a slip of paper. I'm wide awake, and I finished my book. What now? Maybe I'll exercise, take a bath, and try to sleep some more. I'm excited to finally meet the baby!

I'm All That

———— Original Message ————

From: Margot
To: Bert
Subject: I still got it

Dear Bert,

So in case you want to know, I'm "all that" over here.

A handsome Russian dude (they're all gorgeous) came over and started talking to me on the plane from Moscow to Khabarovsk. In Russian of course, so I had no clue what he was saying, but he was making all sorts of eyes at me and everything, so he was obvious. I was in the aisle seat next to this American couple from the Midwest, Robert and Diane Barton. They're pretty cool. Diane knew a few words in Russian, and I only know how to say please and thank you, but the guy just stayed squatting down beside my seat in the aisle, talking Russian. Then he started making "come on" motions, like he wanted me to go sit with him. I guess you can just sit wherever you want? I showed him my wedding ring, and the kids' pictures, but he wasn't dissuaded. He started using lots of hand motions, because obviously we couldn't understand him, and he was getting frustrated. I was wondering why the stewardess didn't tell him to get back in his seat, fasten his seatbelt, etc., but there were evidently no rules on the plane. He just hung around, smiling and trying his best, and Diane and I decided to stop trying to talk and just continue to shake our heads "no." Then he grabbed my hand. Oh my gosh, so I pulled it away fast, and Diane yelled, "Nee-Tro-Guy!" The guy's eyebrows shot halfway up his forehead, then he sheepishly got up and left. Apparently, she said "Don't touch that!" Too funny! Like scolding a little kid. He wandered up and down the aisle a couple times, looking kind of confused and still making eyes at me every time he passed. So I faked sleep, hoping he wouldn't come back. I had my eyes closed and my coat pulled up to my chin like a blanket when I felt something cold on my hand. I opened my eyes, and it was him pressing an orange into my palm.

Diane made so much fun of me, she was brutal, and we were so tired we laughed and laughed like crazy, and then laughed ourselves to sleep, with the help of Robert's Nyquil. After we woke up she kept saying the word orange, like "Orange you hungry?" or "Orange you this or that..."

I'm off to sleep. More next time I get to one of these business centers. Or maybe I'll run off with one of these Russian guys bearing citrus fruit...just kidding. Give kisses to the kids for me.

Love you!

Travelogue First Trip: Problem

~~~6:15 a.m., the next day. Not sure what day it is, jetlagged, maybe Thursday?~~~

Wow, this town is just awful. The broken down project-looking apartment buildings in the freezing cold are sad. Russian buildings here don't have anything like colors, finish work, or landscaping. Not even brick facades. Nothing. Just cement blocks plopped down randomly in the snow. It looks horror-movie-ish. I can't believe people who didn't do anything wrong live in these buildings. There are no houses, only these horrible prison-like structures all over the place. I have to describe them as best I can because I realized this morning that my camera had no film in it the whole trip so far. Oh, well, just when I was wondering what else could go wrong…

They picked me up at 9:00 sharp yesterday morning. We stopped on the way so Luba could go to the city administrator. When she got back in the car, I heard her say in Russian the word "problem" to Andrei more than once. (It's the same word as English.) We pulled up by one of the cement buildings and picked up Anna, my interpreter, a homely girl with a fat masculine face and an attitude. (Ok, so they aren't all gorgeous, just mean-tempered.) I was pretty excited to get to the orphanage, but also literally starving, because my hotel didn't offer any breakfast, just tea. I asked if we could stop and eat on the way to the orphanage and was told no, we were late. Late for what? Is the child going somewhere? Anna and Luba talked and I heard "problem" one or two more times.

When we got to the orphanage, there was indeed a problem. The boy I came to see wasn't there, so we had to leave. It was awful! Later, Anna and I went to the slowest cafe on the planet for dinner. They brought drinks quick enough, but it took them an hour to bring our meals. Luba said she would "solve my problem" while we ate. By the time my chicken came I was exhausted, and maybe even half drunk. Thinking about it, I had had only a bowl of soup all day. I insisted we stop at an internet cafe, where I emailed you about the fiasco at the orphanage. Then back to the hotel for much needed sleep. Just when I was thinking the day couldn't get any worse, I slipped on the ice coming up the hotel steps and fell on my rear end.

I don't know how long I was sleeping before the phone rang. I could barely get up…couldn't shake the sleep off to reach over and pick up the phone…it kept ringing. It was Anna. Luba found an available baby back in Khabarovsk. Can I get on the overnight train in 2 hours? I'd ride alone so that I could spend all day in Khabarovsk and not have to change my return flight. I said ok. What seemed like moments later, there was a knock on the door. It was Anna to pick me up. I had fallen back asleep. I said no, I can't go–I've changed my mind. I was too physically exhausted to raise my head from the pillow. I can't, I told her. My whole body was shaking from the inside. It's not safe for me to ride alone overnight sleeping like a dead woman. She offered to pack my bags for me, but I said no, go home. I must have fallen asleep before she let herself out.

I woke up around 5 a.m. I think she said there was a bus at 8:00 this morning. I don't remember what she said. Was I dreaming? I'm ready. It's 6:45.

Help!

------- Original Message -------

From: Margot
To: Bert
Subject: Help!!

Dear Bert,

There's a real problem here. These morons screwed everything up, and took me to see a disabled kid that isn't the one we saw in our referral video. It's like some type of bait-and-switch scheme, and I'm not falling for it! Call Tanya, call Joseph, and let them know this is bullshit!!!

Earlier today, in the car on the way to see the boy, the interpreter (some kid named Anna from a housing project) looks at me nasty and says in her Boris-and-Natasha accent, "So, Missus, why do you choose disabled child?" So I tell her that I didn't and she says, "Yes, you did. Child is disabled."

"No." I said, "Healthy." I realize I'm talking in one word sentences to make sure she understands me, 'cause now I'm pissed. "Well," she snorts, "child is not healthy. Perhaps you will choose another." What the heck does that mean? I can't just choose another. The agency gives me one choice to accept or reject. It's not like I can shop the orphanage for a kid. What. Is. Going. ON?

I demanded that they pull the car over so we can have a conversation and anyway I was starving and wanted something to eat (and drink. Well, I didn't actually say "drink" but it seemed like maybe a good idea, even though it was only 9:30 in the morning. I think I'm majorly jetlagged.) And she talks to the agent and the driver in Russian and you know what she says to me? She says, "You can discuss when we get to baby house." I wanted to punch her in her pimply face.

We get to the orphanage and they haul out some random little boy. He doesn't look anything like our boy from the referral video. Not even close. It wasn't him. I call for the director, and they bring me an enormous gold-toothed woman in a filthy housedress who introduces herself as the pediatrician. She talks with Luba and Anna in Russian for a while, and I hear the word "autism." So now I'm butting in in English asking what's going on. The pediatrician looks at me and says in English, "Boy is idiot. Will never be normal."

So I said for them to put that boy back, that it's not our boy, that they switched him. I asked where is my boy and they all looked at me like I was crazy, which I might have been at that moment. I said again to put the boy back and they called for someone to come in and take him away. It was awful.

I feel mean, but we don't want to knowingly take on a disabled child, right? We talked about this. But I still feel mean–they made me send some kid away. It's not right. I hate these people.

Anyway, then once the poor kid was dragged away they said they had a "backup," because they suspected I might not take him. Can you believe this? Then they haul in another boy who's like 5 years old and kicking and screaming like a demented animal. And by then I was in crazy-mode, and I said no, take him back. I'm here for a child under 2. They said they have more children available, but the director wouldn't be back until the next day, and only she knew which children were available (I find that hard to believe. Do these people keep no written records?) I was on the verge of having a total conniption.

The rest of the day I was fit to be tied. They took me shopping, for what, I don't know, but I wandered around some store that was right out of some movie about Soviet shortages–unwanted products, empty shelves. They didn't know what to do with me, and I had no idea what to do with myself, either. Thankfully, Anna remembered I was hungry (I had forgotten), and we went for a bowl of soup and then they dumped me back at the hotel to cool my heels for the afternoon. And I wanted to email you then, but the internet was down, so you can imagine I was in a rage.

My on-site agent and the teenage translator returned around 4:30 to say they have only one child, a 4-month-old, available here in town. I could see him, but it would require 2 trips back, because I can't sign for him until he's six months.

Mara Kendahl

We can't afford 2 more trips back! I said no. (And that wasn't all I said!) Now they're "deciding what to do about me" they said. As if I caused any of this!!! Please call Tanya and Joseph right away and have them straighten this out!!!

Travelogue First Trip: Khabarovsk

~~~Khabarovsk, Friday, 6:20 a.m.~~~

Yesterday, I was downstairs early at the hotel "business center" (another wobbly desk with an 80's computer) when Anna called, telling me that there was a problem with the 8 o'clock bus, and that I would be going at 11:00 instead. The problem was that Andrei's car was buried under snow from the previous night's storm. It was blustery last night, and every so often a train passed. I thought it strange that I hadn't noticed the trains the night before. I found out that there weren't trains; it was the storm. I've never heard such fury.

When they finally came to get me, Luba said the Amrex people will be "mad" and the Russian judge will not look favorably on any adoption for me, because my first referral "went bad," and then I "rejected" a boy. Hey, I've also already spent about $15,000, lost days from work, and been taken for a ride. I wasn't going to let them bully me. My original referral didn't go bad. They never let me see our boy! And I didn't reject anyone. Just because they brought a random kid in the room with me doesn't mean the child was a legitimate referral. Does it?

They packed me off on the bus alone, seven hours back through the sub-zero tundra with no one to interpret for me, because Luba wasn't ready to leave. No problem, I had already ridden the bus, I knew the drill, and yet, I had already pre-paid to be accompanied, so this wasn't exactly ok. Again, there were only a handful of people on the whole bus, including the two drivers. How can this be profitable for the bus company? Anyway, Luba put me on the bus like I was a child and talked about me to the lady next to me and to the driver. It was 30 below outside, but on the bus it was like 80 degrees, and I was sweating and taking off all my clothes down to my tshirt. Everyone else stayed bundled up which was the weirdest thing.

When my bus arrived in Khabarovsk, Natasha (same interpreter as before) and Natalia (a new agent to replace Luba since she was still in Komsomolsk-na-Amur) were waiting at the gate, and I didn't show up. They had a big fight with the bus company agents, and almost caused an international incident according to Natasha, but eventually they found me. I was still on the bus, which was parked in the depot, curled in my seat under a pile of clothes, sound asleep.

The Bus Ride Back

──── Original Message ────

From: Margot
To: Bert
Subject: Checking in after a long ride

Dear Bert,

(I wrote this letter on paper while I was on the bus home from my ridiculous trip to Komsomolsk-na-Amur, so I could remember and email it to you later.)

    This bus ride is hours through frozen nowhere, just ice and trees again for miles in every direction. I'm so bored I might die. And I'm traveling alone, because my agent "wasn't ready" to go back to Khabarovsk. Convenient, right, after she's been paid to escort me around this Godforsaken country? Seems she told some random lady in the seat next to me to take care of me.

We stopped about 4 hours into the ride at what might have been a military outpost, but it looked like a boy scout troop rigged it up for a weekend camp out. The lady next to me addressed me for the first time with, "toilet?" It's the same word in Russian. So "da" seemed like a good answer, and off we went. The toilets were disgusting holes in the ground with low tin walls propped up with cement blocks and shower curtains for doors. We had to pay a little troll (maybe it was an old woman) for a couple sheets of toilet paper.

After the bathroom, the lady says, "cafe?" Again, the same word as in English. "Da," I said. In the wooden building across from the toilets, she ordered me a coffee. It was pretty frustrating because I was starving but couldn't read the menu or ask for anything myself. We waited at a small table where the drivers were sitting, and they got served huge plates of meat and noodles and soup. I went nuts pointing and gesturing and the lady smiled and said something to the waiter, so I thought she was hooking me up with that monster bowl of stew, too, but instead they brought me black coffee and 3 small, iced, bread balls. I was so disappointed and hungry I started to cry a little. You know how I get when my blood sugar is low. The drivers noticed, but instead of feeding me, they tried to talk to me. And even though I hated everyone and wished them in the blackest hell at that moment, we all ended up laughing. I was, evidently, answering questions, but not the ones they were asking. Later, the driver took my hand and pointed to my wedding ring with a questioning look. I said, "Da," and he let my hand go. I guess he didn't have any oranges.

On the bus we've been watching snippets of American movies in Russian for like an hour, and the only reason I know that, everyone being about 6 of us on the bus, is that I can't sleep. I'm having actual heart palpitations from the high-octane coffee and sweet bread.

And here's the weirdest part of the ride. About 15 minutes ago, for no reason, we just pulled over to the side of the road in absolute, desolate, frozen miles upon miles of nowhere. What was happening? And I thought, "Oh my God, we've broken down and there's nothing for miles and it's 30 below and maybe we'll have to survive and we'll be forced to eat each other like in that book "Alive" about the plane crash, and…" And then some man in a fur coat and hat gets on the bus. Just gets on and takes a seat. A passenger. At first I didn't realize it was a man because he had about 4 inches of icicles hanging from his mustache and eyebrows, covering his eyes and his whole mouth and chin, and I couldn't tell what was wrong with his face. But that's not the weirdest thing. The weirdest thing–that I can't figure out–is where did he come from? There's nothing but white, untouched forest in every direction as far as I can see.

Anyway, there's a couple hours left on this ride, and I'm exhausted and starving. My heart rate is calming down. I'm going to try to close my eyes a while. Sleep will do me good.

Love,
Margot

Travelogue First Trip: Baby House #2

After the bus ride, they took me to the Intourist Hotel in Khabarovsk. It's not bad, but I think it has dancing girls and God-only-knows what else downstairs in the bar at night. I was exhausted and starving, but no, Natalia wanted to go straight to the orphanage, called Baby House #1, so we did, because no one listens to what I might need to do, like eat, sleep, or pee. But things at Baby House #1 didn't work out either, so we went next to Baby House #2, where I finally met our son.

Found Him

———— Original Message ————

From: Margot
To: Bert
Subject: Found Him!

Dear Bert,

I found our son. He's in Baby House #2 here in Khabarovsk!! I have to write this quick because they're coming back to take me to meet him!

But let me tell you about today They jerked me around a little more this morning, but everything is going to be ok. They took me earlier to see some random boy, again, not the boy in our referral. I wonder what happened to him? And on the way to this Baby House #1 (That's what they call the orphanages over here. *Dom Rebyonka* means orphanage and it translates to Baby House), Natalia (the agent) is going on about how she had to pull strings to get another referral so fast. She said her instructions from Amrex were to send me home, but she went out of her way for me. Liar.

They brought out this big overgrown boy, God bless him, but I was afraid of him, God forgive me. I can only describe the poor little soul as "Stitch" from that Disney movie. He was crawling up the walls and grunting. His head, especially his mouth and teeth, were huge. Like monstrous. I played with him a while, thinking I could learn to love him, but really he was such a terrible brute the way he scrambled around the room snorting. I imagined him terrorizing all of us, like a pit bull, and Hazel running screaming at the very sight of him…I was exhausted and overwhelmed. Natalia asked if I would take him, and I said yes. (Don't worry, I recanted.)

I tried to sleep on it, but I was so upset I couldn't sleep. In the morning, to my surprise, I ran into the Mays and the Bartons (the Americans from the Moscow plane ride) sitting downstairs at breakfast! Excellent! I guess they put all the adopting Americans up in the same hotels. I joined them, and we laughed about all my mishaps, and I told them about my new "son." Robert didn't laugh. He said if I wasn't convinced, I should refuse the boy. He said it was too big a decision to take halfheartedly. If I didn't feel called to parent that boy, I shouldn't do it. He actually sent me up to my room to take a hot bath and pray. When I realized it was ok to say no, I felt like I could breathe again.

Natalia and Natasha came back, I told them the boy would not fit in with my family. And then I felt guilty and ashamed, so I blamed it on you, Bert. I'm sorry.

Anyway, Natalia was furious. Why should she be furious? What do I care about her feelings? She said with her teeth all gritted that she had possibly just one more child available for consideration and that she would be back in 40 minutes to solve "my problem." She said if I didn't take him, I'd have to go home and wait months for another referral. Also, she suspected I had been speaking with the other Americans and forbid me to talk to them. Good luck with that, Natalia.

So she just came back about 20 minutes ago frowning and pissy, with photos of a baby who had just gotten approval that day for adoption (or so she said). She showed me the photos of an angel, the most beautiful baby boy in the world. I knew he was our son the instant I saw the photos. Well, I mean that he's supposed to be our son, I can't tell if he's the boy in our original referral video or not. Maybe he is and maybe he isn't, but it doesn't matter. He has a sweet little round baby face, wispy blond hair, and brown eyes like yours. He's perfect. I loved him instantly. I said, "That's him. Let's go!" They said they'd come back in an hour to take me. I can hardly wait!!

I'll do my best to call when I get back from the orphanage. I'm so excited!!

Wish me luck!

Love,
Margot

Perfect

———— Original Message ————

From: Margot
To: Bert
Subject: I met our son!

Dear Bert,

He's perfect, our son, I met him. He's an angel. I'll tell you the whole story from the beginning, so you can feel like you were here with me.

He lives in Baby House #2, which is literally gross. It's a menacing cement block building with a metal door and few windows on the ground floor and a sour-pee stench. We went into a beige and brown waiting area, a huge long empty room, and waited, and waited, and waited. Finally, a stern-faced lady came from the far end of the room with the most adorable baby boy holding her hand and toddling along beside her. Blond hair sticking up every which way. Dark brown eyes. Mouth full of baby teeth. Chubby face and pouty mouth, and skinny little body in a hand-me-down faded light green onesie that looked like it was meant for a girl. The lady picked him up and deposited him on the floor in front of me like he was a sack of dirt and left.

So this is our son. We looked at each other for a long moment. I loved him right away, this little kid who no one wanted. I want him! You'll love him! He was easy to like, too. He didn't want to play much. He was nervous, but not afraid of me. He wasn't feeling well. I sang to him in English and Spanish. I gave him my watch, and we played at taking turns handing it back and forth to each other. How smart he is! Smiley and friendly and catching on quickly! We rolled a ball to each other, and then I gave him some animal crackers.

Yes, I smuggled in the animal crackers from home. How else to get a kid to like you? Natasha told me I wasn't allowed to feed him, so I relied on my New Jersey roots and got tough on her. I got in her face and told her to look the other way or we'd have a problem. I'll feed a kid if I want to. He ate all the crackers, then played with the box. I can't wait to call you, I can't wait to get the paperwork going, I can't wait to tell the agent to schedule our court date! Our baby is handsome, and lovable, and smart, and strong, and sweet, and friendly. I promised our son that we'd get him out of this pee-and-cabbage-stinking place. I promised him.

His cheeks were angry red, and dry, and cracking, so I smeared cortisone ointment on them. His arms and legs absorbed the entire bottle of hand lotion that was in my purse. I've never seen such dry, scaly skin. He had sores, too. They said it's food allergies, but I don't think so.

There were some other children who had to walk through the room where I was, and I saw a little girl who looked so forlorn, and she tugged at my heart because she looked so much like our own Hazel, brown wavy hair, brown eyes, petite white oval face. I inquired after her, but was told she did not qualify for adoption because she still had a living relative. This relative would not take her out of the orphanage, but would not sign papers releasing her for adoption, either. He felt it was best, Natasha explained, because many Russians believe that Americans come to adopt babies and then "sell them for parts" to rich Americans. What a disgusting idea. This man is going to leave this little soul to grow up in this scuzzy orphanage to save her from the Americans. You know what will happen to her? They'll teach her to cook, clean, and sew until they show her the door at around 16 years old. Most of the boys who grow up here will end up hustlers and the lucky girls will be maids, the unlucky, prostitutes.

Can we contact this man, maybe I can talk to him, I asked. "No." Why not? "Just no. Because no." Can I ask the Director? "You will be making a nuisance of yourself, and perhaps they will not give you Dima." I shut up. By the way, that's what they're calling our son. Dima. No way we're calling him that.

The stern-faced lady came back randomly and took my baby away, but told me to wait. Then, a social worker showed up and told me this story:

One day a woman knocked on a family's apartment door and asked the people inside to watch her son while she went to buy milk. She said a quick "goodbye, Dima" to the baby (Dima is a nickname for Dmitri) and left. And that's it.

I said that can't be it. How did he get from the family to here?

Oh, she said, in that annoyed-disgusted manner they all have over here, and continued. Eventually, the police were called. They wrote a report that a two-month old had been recovered, and they brought him to the hospital. The doctors deemed him six-months old and assigned him a birthday in October. They added Ivanov as a last name (it means "Johnson", I guess they use it like "Doe"), and made out a birth certificate for Dmitri Ivanov, born in Khabarovsk.

After the social worker left, I asked my interpreter what she thought of the story. Was the mother from Khabarovsk? Was his name really Dima? Did his mother mean to come back and instead meet with tragedy? Was there ever such a woman, or did the boy's own family turn him over with a cover story? And so on. She looked away and replied, "Who cares?" These people are something else.

We went back for a second visit later that evening. Our baby had a fever and congestion. He grabbed me tight and slept on my chest for the whole visit, except when we woke him up to give him water. His little blond head was perspiring. His cheeks, though, had completely healed with that one application of cortisone. Joseph, God bless him, had told me to bring basic first aid supplies, because the Russians don't spend that kind of money on the orphans. These kids don't even wear diapers, just rags tied around them.

Natalia told me while we were sitting there with the baby asleep that some "minister of such-and-such" is annoyed that I turned down 3 children and wants to know what's wrong with me and why my husband isn't with me to "handle me." We have been "ordered" to come back 2 days early on our eventual second trip to prove that you, Bert, are in charge and that you approve of the child. Can you believe this? These people suck.

Anyway, back to our son. He was much more animated the next day. The fever had subsided. He remembered the game with the watch, and he ate more animal crackers. He understands when I tell him not to shove all the crackers in his mouth at the same time. He takes the last one out and holds it while he eats what's already in there.

Also, Natalia said the caretakers just switched the poor baby's schedule from 2 naps to only one. He's only 15 months! After playing peekaboo and rolling the ball back and forth, he was visibly tired. He laughed for the first time when I was rocking him up and down. (He is a serious baby and doesn't give up a smile easily.) I can see how alert he is by how he plays. I can't wait to get him home.

One of the toothless elderly workers came in to clean and look around for something, and she started chatting with Natalia. When she left, Natasha translated some of the conversation. "Dima is a favorite here. He will grow up to be a big gangster." I had to choose between punching her in her Russian nose or ignoring her. I ignored.

He fell asleep in my arms. I held his little sleeping body for a while, then I had to give him back. We went to his room full of babies everywhere. He was the handsomest of them all. The room had about 25 decrepit cribs in it, each shoved up against the other in rows. I asked which was his, but it seems it doesn't matter. I laid him sleeping in a stained, rumpled crib, kissed him, and left. How I hated to leave him in that filthy place where no one cares that his cheeks crack and bleed, and no one plays with him, and they use dirty t-shirts for diapers even after I brought two jumbo packs of diapers, and it smells like urine and boiled cabbage all day long.

I can't get the sight of one of the other orphans out of my head. They don't let me see much, they keep us parents in special waiting rooms, and we don't really see the other children, but this one little boy, maybe 3 years old, filthy and blind, kept wandering all over the place. When they'd catch him where he didn't belong, they'd call his name, and he'd grind the heels of his hands to his blind eyes and throw himself backwards onto the floor. He'd launch himself in the air like a movie actor who was shot in the chest and had to propel himself backwards dead. Every time he did this he hit his little head. Hard. Then they'd yell at him and drag his body away across the floor while he howled. This is literally the most horrible place imaginable.

On the flight to Moscow last night, I couldn't stop worrying about our son and wondering what will happen to the little girl who looks like Hazel and how long the blind boy will live.

When Angela met me at the airport, she told me the only document I'm missing for court besides the medical updates is the petition to the court, and our case should be ready in two months. I think Amrex in the US is responsible for all the delays. Tanya said it would be 4-6 months before our court date. Excruciating to wait that long, knowing our baby is sick in that bare room with its rows and rows of dilapidated wooden cribs and stinking mattresses.

After breakfast this morning I walked down Arbat Street. It's a promenade with shops and souvenir stands, not much was open yet, but I made my way to Red Square, the Kremlin (KPYMLYN they spell it), and St. Basil's. For some reason the whole square was cordoned off. I stopped in at a small stone church on the outside corner of the square. It was cozy and smoky and smelled like incense, and they were chanting something. Some ladies were bowing and some were kneeling, occasionally putting their foreheads on the floor. Everyone in there looked absolutely desperate. Come to think of it, there were only women in there praying. I didn't see any men. I stayed a while.

On the walk back to the hotel, my bag felt heavy. I'm tired and my stomach hurts. I want to go home. They're coming to take me to the airport in 1/2 an hour. See you soon, God willing.

Love,
Margot

Travelogue Second Trip: Return to Baby House #2

Day 1 Easter Sunday

Margot, I appreciate the log you kept last time, so I will take a turn now. Easter Sunday 8 p.m. departure. 9 hours 5 minutes, flight arrived 4:25 a.m. Moscow time. Now I'm writing from the hotel in Moscow. It's Monday afternoon.

About 2 hours after landing we arrived at the hotel, $145 a night. Russia is dusty, the cars are dirty, the buildings are all brick and cement. The people are mean and do not smile. The hotel is so-so. We went for a walk on the main strip, we ate at a decent restaurant, the food was great but the waitress was surly. Margot was tired, with the long flight and the 8-hour time difference, so we walked for a little after dinner then returned to the hotel to sleep. We went to bed at around 6 p.m. Russian time and were up at 12 midnight not knowing where to go or what to do. There are no vending machines in the hotel.

Day 2 Monday

Next morning breakfast was gross. Beautiful weather temp 57 degrees. Went to Red Square and the tomb of the unknown soldier and the dead body of the Russian communist leader Lenin. He's a dead body in a glass box, and when I pointed and whispered at how gross his beard and fingernails look, armed guards came and yelled at us in Russian and threw us out. It's funny now, but for a minute it wasn't funny.

At 3 p.m. we called home, 7 a.m. NJ time. Then Angela picked us up for a 6:15 p.m. flight. Plane left at 7:00 for Khabarovsk on a 7 hour and 25-minute ride. We will arrive Wednesday at 8:25 a.m. local time in Khabarovsk.

Day 3 Wednesday

Arrived in Khabarovsk, thank you God. The plane was old, dirty, broken, and smelly. So bad I thought I'd throw up. The plane didn't look like it should be able to fly. But after all it was a smooth ride. Margot made friends with an army border patrol officer. They shared whisky together straight from his bottle. They could not understand each other, but the drinking was going swell. After 3 swigs each, they were soon asleep. When we landed, we deplaned on the runway just like when we got on. A bus older than age itself drove us to the terminal where we waited ½ hour for the luggage and our translators. Again the buildings were old and dirty, worse than the projects. The women were all dressed nicely and were tall and thin and blond with blue or green eyes. The cars, trucks, and busses were pre-1940. Dropped our luggage at the Intourist Hotel, then at 10 a.m. they drove us to see the baby. It doesn't seem real to meet "my son" here. He was very quiet and did not smile, cry, or fuss. We dressed him in a new outfit that Margot and her mom bought. The orphanage building was in a ghetto-like complex like a run-down South Ward housing project. After about an hour, we returned to the hotel hungry and tired. After lunch and a quick nap, we went back to see the baby, who by now Margot had decided to name Richard. He was back in his old outfit in the afternoon, and Margot wasn't happy about it.

~~~3:15 a.m., Thursday, Khabarovsk~~~

Thanks for taking a turn at the journal, Bert.

We woke up about 2 hours ago. Just like last trip, up all night and dead tired all day. We saw "Ricky" yesterday. He seems nervous. They say he is active and social. He apparently doesn't want us to know anything about that.

He looks good, but they shaved his head, which isn't cute. He looks like a mini-inmate dressed in the same outfit he had on both days I saw him in January. We changed him into a cute little set that Mom and I got at Bloomingdales. He looked so cute! His rash looks better, slightly. His shoes, though the same, were two different sizes. One shoe, the size 3, was terribly small. The 4 was ok, but he needs 4 ½s. We'll buy him new shoes today.

We saw him at 11:00 am and he fell asleep. At 4:00 we went again, and he fell asleep again. I was concerned and asked the staff doctor about it. She said he missed his nap and seemed stressed, so they gave him a "mix." They tranquilized him? Ridiculous! And they stole his new clothes! Bastards! But we can't do anything about any of it, so we just nodded and smiled.

On the plane over here, we sat next to a Border Patrol Guard who works on the Amur River. He was nice, but he stank

Mara Kendahl

---

of smoke and food and BO. He spoke hardly any English and me even less Russian. He and I drew pictures for each other to pass the time. I think he guards the border against Chinese coming in, based on his drawings of people with horizontal lines for eyes on the other side of a river. I can't imagine there are hordes of folks trying to get in here. Is it worse in China than here? We drank his brandy and ate my granola bars and peanuts and fell asleep. The guy thought Bert was a total wimp for being visibly horrified by the duct tape holding the plane together and for refusing to take a swig from the bottle. He was making gestures that Bert was feminine, but I pretended not to understand to keep the peace. I saw you, Bert, when you gagged when I drank from the bottle he offered. You are kind of a wimp sometimes, but I love you anyway.

Day 4, still Thursday

I'll take a turn at the journal again. I see what you wrote, and it was disgusting to share a bottle with that smelly guy with his scraggly moustache. I puked in my mouth a little, but I thought we'd die on that jalopy plane, so I didn't want to fight.

We went to bed on Wed at 6 p.m. and woke up at midnight, then slept again at 4:30 a.m., up at 7:30 a.m. Breakfast at the hotel is gross. The eggs look and feel like flan. Off to see our little man at 9:15 a.m. He was quiet but then warmed up to us. He smiled for the first time. We took off his clothes to check him. He had a rash, but we can take care of that. At around noon we left for lunch. We walked in town a while, then returned to the hotel to call home. At 3 p.m. we will be picked up to shop for clothes for the little one. The orphanage staff said we need to bring him shoes and a coat if we want to take him outside to play. After his new clothes disappeared, I'm not happy to buy anything else. I'll buy him everything when we get home where the commies can't steal his stuff.

From our hotel room window we can see the Amur River and some twinkling lights in China on the other side.

Today in the morning we went to a church that Margot said she liked from her last trip. In the afternoon, we returned with a coat and shoes for Ricky, so they let us take him for a walk outside on the building grounds. He played with us for a while in good spirits. When we left, we brought the coat and shoes with us. Dinner at a Japanese restaurant, then bed at around 9:30. I was up at around 2 a.m., Margot at 3:30. It's hard to rally from the jetlag. The time difference is too much. Court today. Keeping my fingers crossed.

Kangaroo Court

*U*ncomfortably upright on a worn wooden bench outside the courtroom sit two dark-haired foreigners, a man and a woman, awkward, conspicuous. The clock above them emits a decrepit t-t-ticking sound in the flickering fluorescent light. The woman squints, confused, at the silent chain gang standing single file down the hallway. All young and handsome, tall and White. A uniformed guard parades in front of them, glaring, his shoes click-clacking on the stone floor. He stops. T-tick, t-tick. The couple is silent, too, communicating in glances, inhaling the ambient unhappiness.

A too-young court-appointed interpreter approaches the couple and speaks their language, English, barely. It's time. The straightening of a tie, the smoothing of a skirt, the swift gathering of belongings, and they proceed into the stark whitewashed courtroom. Presiding at the head of the vast, grey room is a folding table covered in a dirty cloth like an altar of a long-abandoned church. To the right squat two crooked tables, one leaning like a cripple, where three weathered, middle-aged women seem to be arguing. The interpreter ushers the couple to a rickety wooden banister, and they stand at it, unsure. The woman glances behind her where chairs ought to be, and then at her husband. He takes her hand in his. She considers requesting chairs, but the interpreter has joined the other women at the table to the right, 10 yards away. The couple waits, standing.

A door opens. Harsh Russian words precede the entrance of the judge, a lumbering woman in a threadbare brown suit. She deposits herself behind the head table with a curt nod and flings more Russian words out into to the echoing room. The other women take turns doing the same. From her seat across the room, the interpreter calls to the foreigners and explains in rudimentary English that these are the preliminary proceedings and the foreigners are to smile. The foreign woman bares her teeth. The foreign man may not have understood the directive.

The interrogation begins. *In what type of house you live? How much money is your salary?* Each answer the foreigners provide is met with facial contortions. Disdain? Disgust? The foreign man is convinced that the interpreter is not relaying his answers faithfully. Another question: *Why you take child?* A troubled glance passes between the couple. The foreigners begin a tentative explanation, then elaborate, taking turns, trying to be thorough. When they finish, the interpreter speaks a sentence or two. The women at the table to the right look bitter, bored. The judge shakes her head. More questions: *Do they hit child for discipline? What do they feed child? Will child have own room?*

The foreign woman snaps that the boy will not have a room for himself, but rather will share with his soon-to-be brother. She asks, impatience coloring her tone, if it is required that the child have his own room, and if all children in Russia have rooms of their own. At this, the interpreter speaks a while. The foreign man cringes. The foreign woman scratches at her elbows and examines the ceiling.

More questions, the answers to which the judge has in front of her in a bulging file, each page carefully compiled and submitted by the foreign couple over months. Forms, documents, recommendations, background checks; reports from social workers, law enforcement officials, medical professionals; notarizations and confirmations from county clerks and state officials; in duplicate, and translated. Everything is there as required. Each page pristine and unread.

Eventually, the judge orders the couple to wait while the women deliberate, which the foreigners suspect consists of chatter about local current events and recipes for beets. There is no reference to their persons nor their paperwork for the term of the "deliberation."

After an excruciating 22-minute wait, the judge asks the foreigners if they have any last words before her decision. The foreign woman asks if she might take the boy home soon, if the judge might waive the 10 day in-country waiting period. She refers to a recent Russian doctor's report about a possible heart problem, and explains she'd like to get prompt treatment for the boy. As the interpreter relays this, the judge seethes, then barks angrily, looking directly at the foreigners, gesticulating roughly as though they should understand. The interpreter explains that the judge is angry. "She says you don't like health of child. You waste court's time. You go home."

Travelogue Second Trip: Almost Home

Day 5, Friday, Court Date, 4-24-03

At 11:30 after breakfast we were met by the court agent who told us not to try to ask the judge to waive the 10-day waiting period because it makes the judge mad. Who cares? We asked anyway, to no good result. They granted us the baby, but the judge and all the court staff were a joke. They're all in on some game together like we were set up, mafia style. Probably they get kickback money from the hotel when they make us stay 10 extra days. Margot's upset about the waiting period.

We left court at around 2 p.m., and we got lunch, and I stood in line for a haircut. Everyone just stood in line, no one talked to each other. Not like waiting in a barber shop at home where you'll make 10 friends. Here they stood single file; no one said a word. Not one single word. We bought shoes and lotion for the baby. By then it was 4 p.m., time to go and see the little one again.

The temperature here has been beautiful. The food is ok. The people don't have many cars, and even if they did, there aren't any places to park them. The cars are not washed and the streets are full of dust. The buildings are old and in their original condition, poorly maintained, run down. The heat comes from pipes that run through town above ground and there is no control for it to turn it up or down or shut it off. It's hot inside everywhere we go. Also, we have to grease palms all day long. "Gifts" to the orphanage staff, drivers, agents, interpreters, everyone. What a racquet.

Day 6, Saturday

Out at 9 a.m. to see the little Mr. Rick. He is warming up to us. We took him for a walk in the playground outside. There was no one else on the playground. We aren't allowed to be without an interpreter or alone with the baby. Margot says the people she met in January were allowed to bring their babies home right after their court date and stay in the hotel with the baby during the whole 10-day waiting period. We aren't allowed to take him anywhere, though, and they won't let us take him to our hotel even for the day until the entire 10-day period is over.

Back at the hotel by 12 noon, then dinner at a Russian restaurant. At the restaurant you have to pay for everything. A lemon for my water is an upcharge. So is a sugar cube or a pat of butter. The napkins are all 4 inch one-ply squares of tissue paper that don't absorb anything, and they won't give you another one. Every waitress hates us.

Tomorrow I'll go home, and Margot will stay alone in the hotel for 10 days doing nothing before she and Ricky can fly home. Better her than me, I'm at the end of my patience wasting time here. This all could have been done in a day and a half.

Black and Proud

———— Original Message ————

From: Margot
To: Mom
Subject: from your newly designated African-American daughter

Dear Mom,

Bert emailed to say he got home safe and sound and found a clean house and happy kids. Thanks sooo much for helping Winifred with the kids while we were away. It was a load off our shoulders to know you both had everything under control. You guys are the best! Sorry I didn't email earlier, but the internet hasn't been working here for a couple days.

 The adoption was granted, as I'm sure Bert told you by now. But it's been like a comic tragedy from day one over here. I have to tell you about the court. Dad will love this, too. The whole courtroom thing, I'm pretty sure, was fake. We were in there for-like-ever, and the interpreter was basically no help at all. She told us at one point to smile while the judge was spouting some nonsense that no one bothered to translate for us. But here's the best part–the judge had a full blown hissy fit in the courtroom when I asked her to waive the 10-day waiting period. I don't know what the heck the waiting period accomplishes, except to make people spend more money and pay their translators and give more "gifts" which are basically mandatory bribes. I have to stay in this stinking hotel and eat their gross food off their chipped dishes and pay extra for a wedge of lemon for my tea and extra again for a packet of sugar to keep my blood sugar up so I don't kill someone.

Anyway, thankfully the adoption is a done deal, and I can't wait for you to meet Ricky! You'll love him! Bert told me he told you all about him and showed you pictures already. This is so exciting! But being here stinks.

Let me get back to how ridiculous court was. So in court the judge had a conniption when I asked about the waiting period. I told her one of the examining doctors said Ricky might have some type of heart murmur or something, so I figured we should get some medical attention at home sooner rather than later. So I asked. And you know what the phony judge does? She sends us home. Home? Home my ass. Six months of paperwork, two trips to Russia, and by now close to $25,000 in fees, and she's pissed because I make a simple request in the kid's best interest? Seriously, I could have killed her in that ugly commie suit and all her vicious cronies, too. I wanted to ask her what Russia would do if good Americans stopped coming to pick up some of their 600,000 orphans in the Russian system. Right? I wanted to ask her how many children she adopted.

But I didn't say any of that because that joke of an interpreter clearly wasn't doing her job, so why bother? Is a judge even supposed to get personally offended? So Bert speaks up, and it took a while to soothe the judge, I wasn't helping at all, and finally she granted the adoption but kept the 10-day waiting period in effect. That meant one of us has to stay in town for 10 more ridiculous days. One meaning me. And they wouldn't even grant us custody until the end of the 10 days! So I'm staying in the hotel alone while my legal son stays in the orphanage. This is some serious BS.

So here I am in this raggedy gross hotel room that hasn't been redecorated since ever, bored for 24 hours straight so that I know for real what "bored to tears" means. I read all my books, can't understand crap on the TV, and I already knitted a hat for the baby and ripped it out and knitted it again with the same yarn, because there's nowhere to go for more yarn. And every day I call the interpreter, not the court interpreter, the other one, (Natasha) to call Natalia (my agent, the one we gave a gift to because the agency told us we have to give gifts, and she said she didn't like it!) to come get me and take me to the orphanage to visit, because if I skip a visit they can get quote unquote angry according to her and revoke the adoption.

But here's some more BS. They don't always let me in. I have to bring a gift every day though, like diapers or wipes or baby ointment or shampoo. Better not forget that gift! They take the gift first, then shut the door and leave me standing there while they decide if I can come in. Oh, and I keep bringing packs of diapers, but each time they let me in they've got Ricky's little ass tied up in a grimy t-shirt for a diaper. Even though I brought a whole package the day before! Stinking lousy place looks like some Charles Dickens novel, smells like boiled vinegar, full of toothless women and kids in rags. They go in with my gift and come back later while I'm still waiting like a moron at the door and tell me he's sleeping or he's got a cold or they're too busy. But the other American family--the farmers from the Midwest? When I saw them in the dining room at breakfast we talked briefly (we're not "allowed" to talk, their interpreter yells at them to hurry if she sees us), and they said they're allowed to take their baby out for the day, and no one gives them grief. And they shared a bit of gossip their interpreter told them, that there's evidently an African-American family here to adopt, and all the folks at the orphanage are upset that one of the babies is going to be Black. They said that "the administration," whoever that is, tried to block the adoption but the court approved it anyway. Can you believe these people? As if the baby's going to be Black. And even if it were going to actually be Black, who cares? So the farmers tell me to cheer up, it could be worse. They said they've been praying for the African-American family, though they haven't run into them yet, and now they'll pray for me, too.

So I ask my interpreter about it in the car on the way to the orphanage and she looks at me like I have two heads. "You're Black," she told me. I felt like I was on Candid Camera, that show from when I was a kid. I half expected the driver to turn around, and shout "Smile!" and we'd all have a good laugh. But that didn't happen. I mean, I get it that they don't know what to make of Bert being Hispanic, and I get it that I'm petite and have dark hair, unlike these big blonds over here. I get it that most of the Americans coming to adopt are Midwesterners and farm folk who look and talk differently from us New Jerseyans, but do they really think that our darker features make us African-American? C'mon...

And then I realize I'm staring at her, and my mouth is hanging open, and I react with, "I'm not Black." And she says quite matter-of-fact, "Yes, you are. You and your husband are Black." I felt like I was going insane. It was surreal, and I tasted anger in my throat. So wrong for so many reasons! Because why would she care if we *were* Black? And I immediately wanted to take back what I said, to say, *Hell, yeah, I'm Black!* because whatever it is about me that they don't like, I'm proud of it. If being "Black" makes them not like me, then I want to be Black, and I'm proud to be Black. How dare they?! I'm proud to be every kind and color of person that these animals don't like.

So I don't know what else to say about that, except that I can't wait to get my Black ass and my little Black baby home. I miss you guys so much!

Natalia's Bibles

The black family is different from other Americans. Others white, big, loud, with bibles. Today blacks give me bottle of whisky like gift, but Russians like vodka I say. Black man says in America when you receive gift, you say thank you. Even if you don't like it, black lady says. I tell them I do not like whisky, but is better gift than what other Americans bring. Bibles. Always bibles. I have many bibles, different sizes, colors, English, Russian. The blacks say read one, but I don't. Fairy tales. I start once to read, and so many names, more than Dostoyevsky. No author on bible. Dostoyevsky is proud of his great works and signs his name. Not bible author. He hides. The black man walks away, but black lady listens. She says to me sell bibles. I do not own shop. I tell her I need shop to sell. But she tells other ways to sell. She says if I sell, someone buys. She called this in English win-win. I get money I want, and people get bibles they want. But idea is bad for me, because I must work to sell. I do not want more work. Bibles are free gift. Not free if I work. She says OK, donate to church, and be happy rid of bibles. But I have to carry bibles to church, for nothing. This is not win-win, because every time more Americans come, Americans bring more bibles, bibles, bibles. I lose.

Fairy Tale Part 3: Damaged

*H*appiness soon faded because poor Ricky was sick and suffering, and that made everyone sad. Lots of doctors tried to help Ricky, but he didn't get better. His body and his brain were damaged from the alcohol his first mommy drank while she was pregnant with him.

Hey, Blogosphere!

This blog is brand new today. Welcome! -- though I'm not sure who'd be interested in reading posts of me blowing off steam. Honestly, I foresee this blog becoming one long rant. Because I need to have a rant right about now. Honestly, I need to have a rant most days…

So I'm brand spanking new at blogging, and I'm starting this blog to talk about my son for a few reasons: 1, because no one else wants to hear it; 2, because therapy's not an option (I'm out of time and money), and 3, I feel the need to talk. About Ricky. That's my son. He is the sweetest little angel and a good, smart boy who tries hard to please, but doesn't always succeed. He's adorably quirky. He enjoys "new music" like works by Harry Partch and John Cage, and he loves to eat multicolored salads color by color. His favorite toy is a plastic rat, and he wants to be an archeologist one day. And he's a little bit nutty. A lot nutty. He's mentally disabled.

Ricky is almost 9 years old. I want to write down some of the crazy stuff that happens around here, as well as a little history of the craziness for the last 7 1/2 years. I don't tell my friends much about what goes on because who wants to hear crazy all the time? No one wants to hear it, and no one understands it. That's why I have you now, my dear blank blog page. And anyway, because Ricky is handsome, well spoken, and well- mannered in public (he can hold it together for short periods of time under supervision) people don't always entirely believe me. That's irritating. I promise right now that there will be no fiction here.

Let me start by writing a little about my Ricky. We adopted him when he was 1 1/2 years old. An adorable blond baby, but in poor health because of the primitive conditions at the orphanage in Russia. The place was a filthy dump and stank like cabbage. We were told he was healthy. That was the big lie that changed our lives forever. Whose lives, you ask? There's me, Bert, and our two (biological) kids, who were just 4 1/2 and 3 at the time. If we already had two healthy kids, why did we adopt? That's a story for another night. But the short sweet version is that there are tons of kids out there in the world alone, and it seemed like the right thing to do.

So the adoption process was grueling, and the Russians were horrible jerks the whole way through. I know some people had positive experiences adopting from Russia, but we are not those people. Ricky got home and immediately had problems adjusting. He would cry and scream with no provocation whatsoever. He had health problems. He was scrawny (malnourished at the orphanage, but ate like a champ at home) and couldn't gain weight. Our treks to doctors began. We saw every kind of doctor you can imagine, and ran every test, no matter how implausible, including genetic testing. Each doctor came back with a similar report: "Yeah, there's something wrong, but we don't know what it is." Um, thanks. There was one nasty doctor in particular who decided that the only thing wrong with Ricky was me taking him to so many doctors. What an ass!

So fast forward. Ultimately, after years, we get a diagnosis of FAS. That's Fetal Alcohol Syndrome. I don't know why the heck they call it "fetal" because it affects the fetus from the time it's a fetus until the time it is a full grown person, and forever. They should call it Permanent and Forever Alcohol Syndrome. Let me give you some facts:

- It is the leading known cause of mental retardation in western civilization (National Institute of Health).
- Of all the substances of abuse, including heroin, cocaine, and marijuana, alcohol produces by far the most serious neurobehavioral effects in the fetus, resulting in permanent disorders of memory function, impulse control, and judgment. (Institute of Medicine Report to Congress, 1996).
- Among children with FAS…up to age 15, the social maturation process seems to be stunted at the level of a six-year-old child (Alcohol Clinical Exp Research, 1998).
- Fewer than 10% of individuals with FAS are able to successfully live and work independently (Center for Disease Control and Prevention, 1996).

Yeah, it's pretty bad. (And weird that I can cite sources off the top of my head, right?)

Want some more?:

Elementary school children with FAS usually exhibit characteristics such as attention deficits, hyperactivity, language difficulties, learning disabilities, cognitive disabilities, memory difficulties, poor impulse control (lying, stealing or defiant acts), small size, and social difficulties (overly friendly, immaturity, easily influenced, and difficulty with choices.)

And the craziness Dr. Patel (Ricky's specialist) says is in store when Ricky hits puberty is, well, crazy. I don't believe Patel has a crystal ball, but he said Ricky will have trouble with "executive function." That means he won't understand cause and effect, so he won't learn from his mistakes. He won't quite grasp the concepts of time or money. He'll have trouble remembering information and processing the information he does remember. It'll be hard for him to self-monitor his behavior and self-regulate his emotions without assistance. His moods will be prone to swinging from high to low, and he'll need assistance to compose himself. He will likely not have much internal motivation, nor a sense of remorse when he's done wrong. It sounds like a nightmare, and I don't want to believe it. But so far, Patel's been mostly right.

Patel said trouble with executive function leads to things like violent crime, fire setting, molesting, incarceration, joblessness and stealing. As you might suspect, I hate going to see Dr. Patel.

Anyway, enough for one day. Thanks for listening? --reading? See you tomorrow.

Jungle Gym Fun

Hey, Blogosphere, I am having a crappy crappy night, because my son, who is living in Puerto Rico right now (long story, I'll get to it in a few days) is having a birthday party that his aunt arranged. But evidently, she forgot to invite his friends. What?! I am furious!! I think she's at her wits' end with him, and he's going to have to come home.

Anyway, that is not what I want to rant about tonight, because it will just end up being an uninformed rant, because I'm not quite sure what's going on. My husband is in PR now with Ricky, and he's probably going to bring him home in a few days if we can't get this all straightened out. But I haven't even explained what I'm talking about, so more about that in another post.

Right now, I'm frustrated! When I get wild like this, it reminds me of that one moment when Ricky was 4, when I realized that something was way more wrong than anyone suspected, and I was angry and sad and frustrated and scared all at once. This moment haunts me, especially when I'm stressed out. It was the moment I knew everything was going to change. Previously, we thought Ricky was just "a handful" or "acting up" or "having trouble adjusting." Wrong. That moment he was free-falling through the air? The wild look on his face told all. It's like the world flickered and went dark for a split second while I was watching, and when the light regained normalcy, nothing was ever normal again.

It was February. We were on a family vacation, Bert, me, and the three kids. We went to San Antonio, Texas, for winter break to see a rodeo. We're not country people (We live in suburban NJ just a quick jaunt from NYC), but it sounded like fun, so we went. Ricky by this time was taking a medication called Tenex that was supposed to help him "organize his thoughts" according to his psychiatrist, Dr. Burns. (This was before we discovered Dr. Patel.) She had labeled him as Oppositional-Defiant and ADHD, with Mood Disorder, Conduct Disorder, and possible Early Onset Bipolar Disorder. But all of it, supposedly, was going to be fixed with counseling and medication. Right.

Ricky completely ruined the vacation. Every moment was spent managing his behavior. And that drove the rest of us crazy, and we bickered with each other. A lot. It was awful.

One day in the car Ricky was having another rage-over-nothing in his car seat. (He was not tired, hungry, thirsty, wet, soiled, nor fighting with anyone over anything. I checked.) He was just raging and flailing himself around and shrieking and driving all of us to distraction. Bert pulled the car over at a local park and let the kids out to run around and play on the jungle-gym, hoping Ricky would blow off some steam. All three kids scrambled out and climbed up to the top of the jungle-gym.

Alex swung around like a monkey and climbed back down, then ran around. Hazel slid down the slide, then climbed back up for another slide. Ricky climbed to the top of the jungle gym, then launched himself straight up into the air out over the park like a bird taking off. I saw his face. He looked insane. There is no other way to describe the look on his face. Just insane. (In truth, I may have looked a little crazy at that

moment, too.) He landed on the ground flat on his face before I could reach him. He popped right up, with pebbles embedded in his cheeks and blood trickling down his nose. He jumped up clapping and spun around wildly screaming "More, more!" and raced to climb back up.

I knew then that this was bigger than I had imagined. Anyone who saw him at that moment would have known there was some serious damage in that child. This is not just a difficult kid. This is something terrifying.

P.S. As always, I called the Dr. Burns for guidance. She said don't let him play on any more jungle-gyms. Gee, thanks, I never would have thought of that.

P.P.S. San Antonio's rodeo is cool. I'd like to go again someday.

Notes for the DDD

*P**er the request for an in-depth report of our social and medical "journey" with Ricky, following are notes to share with the case worker from the Division of Developmental Disabilities, appointment tomorrow, 3:00 p.m., here. Duplicate copies for files.*

• • •

Dr. Petrikov, a Russian-born pediatrician examined Ricky upon arrival to the US and said, "This child is bad. He has a mean little smile. You never should adopt any child from Russia. They are in the orphanage for a reason. Parents are of bad stock, criminals, prostitutes, alcoholics. The child is a throwaway. Why would you want to pick up someone else's throw aways?" That was the last time we ever went to her office.

The new pediatrician, Dr. Carson, realized something was wrong with Ricky's growth and development, but had no idea what. I started to ask for referrals to specialists, which came grudgingly.

During this same time, Ricky was registered in a nursery school, Zora's, that was excellent and dealt with whatever behavior Ricky presented. After school he was enrolled in a gymnastics class at a local gym to expend some of his extra energy. He did well the first two classes. By the third class, the instructor complained that Ricky did not listen to instructions. By the fourth class she said that he simply did whatever he wanted to do during class time, paying no mind to her whatsoever. In the 5th class, he was so wild he injured a classmate. We were asked not to return. I enrolled him at the YMCA in a swimming class. He behaved similarly there and was removed from the class.

Child-psychologist, Dr. Doralee, did play therapy with Ricky once a week at the Children's Hospital. She didn't do anything different from what I did with him; played legos, coloring, pegs in holes, etc. She talked to him, and explained why his behavior wasn't nice. Yeah, like no one ever told him that before. I was frustrated.

I asked for another therapist, and got Dr. Weiss. I don't know what Ricky and Dr. Weiss did, because the visits required that I wait in the hallway. Alex, Hazel, and I waited in the hallway for an hour once a week. Dr. Weiss reported that Ricky behaved poorly because he felt bad inside. That doesn't make sense to me, nor is it helpful. I asked Dr. Weiss for behavior plans, strategies, techniques to implement. Week after week, I was given nothing, and was told only that Ricky "feels bad." Ok, enough of this nonsense. I stuck with it for over six months, then called it quits with Dr. Weiss. Also, his accent was so thick, I could barely understand him. I wonder if Ricky understood him. What was Ricky possibly getting out of these visits?

By the time Ricky was two, I called the State of NJ for Early Intervention Services. They agreed he qualified for service and came to our home twice a week. He had occupational therapy for sensory integration dysfunction, and general education therapy, just to bring his behavior and learning up to speed. I was thrilled to have a diagnosis. Sensory integration dysfunction! I read everything I could about it. We bought a special soft brush, and brushed his whole body with it three times a day. We got boxes to fill with dry rice, dry beans, water, clay, everything that he could touch and manipulate, to help alleviate this new-found dysfunction. We were careful with noises, bright lights, shirt tags, socks that might be too big, etc. We missed going to the circus that year, because it might be overwhelming for him. Nothing seemed to change him in the least, but we latched on to the hope that this sensory integration thing was causing problems, and the whole family adapted in the hopes of helping Ricky.

Meanwhile, Ricky was still as skinny as a rail, no matter what or how much he ate. We started our round of specialists.

Dr. Morris, reputed to be an excellent pediatric gastroenterologist, was initially alarmed at Ricky's physical presentation, said so, and ordered tests. After a few blood tests and 20+ stool samples, Morris found Giardia in Ricky's stool sample. Ricky had to go on a month's round of strong antibiotics. In fact, Dr. Morris put the whole family on the month's worth of antibiotics, because he said we could all have the parasite since we share food. We were thrilled. This was the cause of his failure to thrive! A parasite! Kill it, kill it!! Once he could get proper nutrition, his brain would function properly, he would grow, he'd be healthy, his sensory problems would disappear. We willingly sucked down those antibiotics for a month. After the antibiotics,

Ricky would plump up, according to the doctor, and there would be a marked change in his behavior. We waited. And waited. I called the doctor. He said to wait a couple months. I did. After 3 months of waiting, we went back to his office. Ricky had gained only a few ounces since our last visit. At this point, Dr. Morris said there was nothing at all wrong with the child, and that I was a neurotic mother. I should let him be the size and shape that he will, and stop focusing on perfection. I argued that he was the one who had been alarmed at Ricky's size, and that he had used the word "alarmed." He ordered me out of his office. I said he couldn't throw me out, I was firing him. A couple years later, I read his medical notes, which included the words "overly aggressive mother" and his diagnosis that the child was healthy.

After the fiasco at Dr. Morris's, we went to Dr. Sario, another gastroenterologist, who ran all the same tests and a few more. He put Ricky on Prevacid for constant belching, which began after the round of antibiotics from Dr. Morris.

He also sent us to a nutritionist, Dr. Nelson, who put Ricky on a special diet. Ricky immediately gained 1 3/4 lbs! It was his diet! The whole family went on Ricky's health food diet. We were happy to have found the cause of his problems. New diet, here we come! But a week later, the weight gain stopped suddenly. Then, Ricky began to lose weight. The nutritionist had no explanation and said she had never seen such a thing in a child.

The nutritionist sent us to an allergist, Dr. Black, who tested Ricky and found no allergies. By this time, Ricky had lost 1 1/4 pounds. The nutritionist suggested he go back on his regular diet, and sent us back to Dr. Sario, who then did an endoscopy, and found H. Pylori in Ricky's stomach. New hope! More treatments. And nothing.

We went to see a team of genetic specialists. The doctors were alarmed at his presentation. Ran all tests. Nothing.

We went to see an endocrinologist, Dr. Chin. Doctor was sure something must be wrong. Ran all tests. Nothing. In the waiting room, I read an article about how heart problems sometimes cause physical and emotional problems in children.

We went to see a cardiologist, Dr Reinhardt. Ran all tests. Innocent heart murmur, and nothing more. Told us we never had to return, there were no cardiac issues.

We went to see a neurologist, Dr. Lombard. This elderly doctor examined Ricky and said, "You definitely have a problem here. I want to tell you that. Don't let anyone say there is no problem. I don't know what the problem is, though. But there is one, so keep at it." This was the first affirmation from any professional that confirmed what I knew–that there was a problem, but no one had found it yet. He suggested Ricky see a psychiatrist.

By now, Ricky was "aging-out" of the Early Intervention System. He would no longer be eligible on his 3rd birthday, and we would have to apply for occupational and general education therapy through the school system. At his last appointment with his physical therapist, he was so defiant, that the therapist stormed out early. She said she had been "doing this a long time," and had never met a more "coldly defiant child" as my son. She suggested we not bother applying for occupational therapy or general ed through the school system, because if a child won't participate in the treatment plan properly, it is simply a waste of time. She, too, suggested a psychiatrist.

We went to see Dr. Burns, a psychiatrist with Children's Hospital. She diagnosed ADHD and possibly Childhood Manic Depression. She put him on his first prescription, Tenex. It calmed him down a little. We needed to have his blood pressure monitored bi-weekly, so I went to Dr. Carson's office for that. After the first time, Dr. Carson said she would not monitor his blood pressure. I could not understand why. I was paying for the visit. She said she disagreed with the medication, and if Dr. Burns wanted his blood pressure taken, she could do it herself.

I switched all three children to another pediatrician, Dr. Kelly, with the local medical group. We stayed with Dr. Burns and the Tenex medication for over a year. Still, I knew this was not the answer. At first the Tenex calmed him down. But he soon became used to it. We increased the dosages. After about a year, we were back where we started pre-Tenex, or worse.

After Ricky injured himself in a troubling incident on vacation in Texas, I spoke to Dr. Burns and told her we needed to make changes. Then, she added Oppositional Defiance Disorder, Mood Disorder, Conduct Disorder, and possible Early Onset Bipolar Disorder and OCD to her earlier diagnosis of ADHD and Childhood Manic Depression. Not great news, but at least it was a diagnosis, one that could be managed with the proper medication and monitoring. I read everything there was to read on the matters, and became convinced that Ricky was not bipolar. But I, obviously, am not the doctor. I voiced my concerns and explained why I disagreed with her, but she insisted.

I went back to the kindly old neurologist, Dr. Lombard. I told him of the past 1 1/2 years, and the current diagnosis. He, too, disagreed with the psychiatrist. Here are the notes from the visit with Dr. Lombard:

> Richard was seen by me in August of 2004. He is now 4 years 4 months of age. At that time, he was felt to have oppositional defiant behavior and possible attention deficit hyperactivity disorder. Subsequently, he went for psychological counseling. His mother was not happy with this because she was not given a behavior management plan and the therapist just played and did talk therapy with him, and indeed, it did not help much. She therefore stopped the therapy. She went to Dr. Burns who started him on Tenex, one-quarter of a tablet per day. This worked well, but it is no longer working, even though it is now being given twice a day.
>
> Richard's mother describes him as manic and unable to calm. He is constantly in motion and "feels no pain." He is in a pre-K program and that will continue for another year, as he is not behaviorally ready for kindergarten. His mother is concerned by his behavior which seems to be worsening, although he can be calm at times. It is not clear why there are these alterations in his behavior.
>
> I reviewed the Vanderbilt Rating Scale with his mother, and he is definitely positive for attention deficit hyperactivity disorder, but also for oppositional

defiant disorder, for which he is strongly positive with 8 out of 8 positive symptoms as often or very often.

Richard continues to be a small child with ongoing short stature issues.

Dr. Lombard then goes on to respectfully disagree with Dr. Burns's bipolar diagnosis, changes Ricky's medication from Tenex to Clonidine, and refers us back to Dr. Burns.

At this time, I applied to the school system for help. I also abandoned my career. I could no longer work full time and manage Ricky's therapies, medications, and behaviors.

Dr. Burns suggested Ricky start behavior therapy again, so we went to Dr. Horowitz.

I suspect we were his first patients. He was brand spanking new at Children's Hospital. I began my run down of all the doctors we had seen, all the therapy, all the behaviors, and all the disappointments. Dr. Horowitz ordered all the files from all the doctors I wrote down for him. He took everything home and pored over it for days. The following week he said "When you are a hammer, everything looks like a nail." I didn't know what that meant. He explained that so far, everyone only looked at Ricky based on his or her own specialty. He said that Russian adoptees with behavior problems were quite often the result of brain damage from alcohol consumption, and asked if anyone had mentioned Fetal Alcohol Syndrome as a possibility? I said no. He sent us to Dr. Patel at the FAS Clinic.

Everyone's A Hammer

Another waiting room. Here we are again, florescent lights and chunky women in scrubs and weary moms ignoring their kids as they fuss and roll around on dirty floors. Some kids run, some make foul noises, some whine. Mine won't run around today. He hangs on me. Sitting on my lap, he looks around the room for one brief moment. Then he squirms. And squirms and wiggles and babbles. I release him, but he shakes his cherubic blond head no, hard, and squirms some more, throwing his skinny arms around my neck and scratching at my shoulders as if he wants to climb up and sit on my head.

Finally, he wanders around the room. He squares up to a large woman in a loud floral dress. She is older, African-American, and people might view her and her dress as unattractive. He points at her and shouts, "Mama, why is this big black man wearing a dress?" Silence. She looks at Ricky, and he stares back at her, chin out in defiance. He doesn't like incongruence. More silence. I see from the corner of my eye that she turns to look at me. I'm looking at the magazine in my lap like it's my job. After all, we're sitting in a Children's Hospital in the Psychiatry Department. Is she waiting for an apology? I don't raise my head to look at her or anyone else. Hot anger bubbles into my throat; it's that woman's fault for looking like a dude in that dress. Angry that I'm in another waiting room, waiting, again. But no, it's no one's fault. I know that. I must find something to do with my anger. I snatch a tattered magazine from the germ-infested waiting room table. Ugh, everyone's crazy kids have slimed their greasy hands all over these tables and magazines. And their snotty noses and drooly mouths….How 'bout some sudoku? I flipped to the back. No puzzles. I searched my bag for something to do, then spent the rest of the wait doodling on the back of a denied insurance claim.

After what seems like hours, we're called, and we see a Hasidic Jewish doctor who looks about 15 years old. I know the drill, I've met dozens of doctors. I shake his hand and introduce myself and my son and pretend that I believe he's a professional who's going to help us. The doctor, after shaking my hand, asks me to please never shake his hand again, because it is against the rules of his religion. Oh, for chrissakes!

This doctor has been out of med school for about 5 minutes. Maybe six. He asks for permission to gather all Ricky's files from my long list of doctors. He promises to review everything. Everything. Which means he has nothing to do. A rookie looking for a case. That's ok with me. We've got nothing to lose.

Two weeks later, he calls and explains that all the other doctors are hammers, and when you're a hammer, everything looks like a nail. So, the psychologist found a psychological problem. The allergist found allergies. The cardiologist diagnosed a murmur. The gastroenterologist detected digestive issues. And on and on. Hmmm, this guy seems thorough. He went on to state his conviction that Ricky has brain damage from alcohol exposure in the womb, and recommended we see a Fetal Alcohol Syndrome specialist, Dr. Patel.

Well, wouldn't this be something? I had no confidence in this guy, and he came through with a lead. This guy Horowitz was my last stop. And now he's pointed in a possible direction. Maybe this Dr. Patel will know something.

What a relief to have a possible diagnosis!…wait, but does he really mean brain damage?

48 Out of 50

Hey Blogosphere, today was a Dr. Patel day. Just fooling with Ricky's medication, as always. I see Patel more often than I see my friends. Ugh, I hate going there.

The first time we went to see Dr. Patel was a real turning point. It started the same as always. Sit in the waiting room, fill in forms, complete evaluations, watch as they play with Ricky and put him through their stupid little tests. But it soon became evident that Dr. Patel and his assistant, Dr. Lotti, not only understood my strange answers to their standard intake questions, but they knew what questions to ask. They understood Ricky had symptoms of ADHD, but could sit quietly in one place entertained by a speck on his clothes for long periods of time. They understood his immediate obedience and willingness to please, only to go ahead 30 seconds later and disobey again. The mood swings, the food hoarding, the inconsistency, the indifference to toys, people, praise, and punishment. They started explaining his behavior, telling me how he behaved in certain situations before I could. I told them, "I can't believe it:

it's like you've been peeking in my window the past few years. How can you know him so well?" I continued to complete the lengthy evaluation while they took Ricky into another room to weigh and measure him and examine his face with a special computer program. After they scored my evaluation and finished their exam, they explained to me that they believe he has FAS, which is Fetal Alcohol Syndrome. And because they didn't seem baffled like all the other doctors I've seen, I was willing to almost believe them. They reviewed all their different tests, including my evaluation, on which Ricky scored a 48 out of 50 for FAS. I asked, with hope springing eternal, what were the 2 points he missed. "The confession of the birth mother that she is an alcoholic or that she drank alcohol during pregnancy." Oh.

I was not wary, as I had been in the past, when these doctors handed down their diagnosis. These guys understood my son inside and out. The other doctors had always been off the mark somehow, and it showed immediately. These doctors were right on the money.

Even though they explained that FAS was damage done to the brain in-utero, I was pleased at the time that it was FETAL alcohol syndrome. Sounds like something he should grow out of soon. I wasn't hearing them that this was a lifelong struggle, that it was brain damage, that he would never be healed. I still believed that there was some kind of therapy that I could obtain. We could work at it, and with time and effort this would all get better. But still, brain damage was quite a blow. I was relieved to have a believable diagnosis and a team of experts at my back, but brain damage and mental disability was much more than I had anticipated. We went from behavior difficulties and possible illnesses (curable) to mental disability and brain damage (not curable). Nasty to finally get a diagnosis and then have all hope of any cure yanked away. At the time, I held on to the belief that working with Patel and Lotti could make everything better somehow.

I got a call from a girlfriend while I was crying in the car on the way home from that first visit with Patel. She asked how the appointment went, and if I was ok. I told her the doctors thought my son was permanently mentally disabled. She was supportive and invited me over for a cup of coffee before we had to pick up our kids at school. Over coffee, I tried to understand and explain what Patel had told me. Her husband was milling around the kitchen while we were talking. He said, "Don't worry, there will be a place for him in the world. Someone has to get the shopping carts from the parking lot and put them back in a row." That hurt.

I got this follow up report in the mail from Patel's office, and I have an e-copy that I'll post here, in case anyone's reading.

> This s a 4 1/2-year-old male who presents today accompanied by adoptive mother for initial neurodevelopmental evaluation. Major concerns today revolve around Richard's difficulty with behavior and attitude. He exhibits significant mood swings, distractibility, irritability, and does not play well with other children. He has previously been diagnosed with Mood

Disorder, possible Bipolar Disorder, ADHD, and Oppositional Disorder. His current medication regime includes Tenex.

Home behaviors reveal that on different days, Richard can be a different person, whose abilities are great, but he needs to be monitored to follow through on directions. He does have some atypical behaviors, where he will pick at his fingers and cuticles and other objects all day, and he will cry all the time. He has no specific fears, and no specific likes or favorite toys, objects, or people.

Appetite is somewhat problematic, where he has always had difficulty with weight gain, and has hidden food in his mouth previously. He is not particular about the foods that he eats, and it all depends on his mood for the day.

Sleeping is not reported as problematic. He goes to bed at 8 p.m., and will sleep through the nights without difficulty. This may be due to his medication.

Social skills are problematic. He can be unpleasant, whiny and manipulative. It is reported that he is having difficulty with behaviors in Sunday School, and although he is invited to play dates, he is never invited back again. He has an older brother, Alex, who is 7 years old, and an older sister, Hazel, who is 6 years old. Although he is connected, especially with Hazel, his older siblings lose their patience with him because he can be quite annoying. He does great with one-on-one, but shows significant behavioral difficulties in group settings. He has participated in organized sports and was asked not to return.

Background History: Background history reveals that Richard was adopted from Russia at 19 months of age. He did spend approximately 6 months in a pediatric hospital and 6 months in an orphanage prior to being adopted. Mom did adopt Richard at 19 months of age, where she reports that for the first month, he slept significantly, and then began significant crying behaviors. He was evaluated by Early Intervention, and did receive some therapies for clumsiness and out of control behavior. He had been evaluated for preschool, but it was reported that they deemed services unnecessary due to behavioral problems vs. physical or educational problems.

Development: It is reported that he always had difficulty with visual pursuits, and does not really show a social smile. It is unknown when he spoke his first words, but was speaking in sentences by 20 months of age. Toilet training occurred at 9 months of age.

Gross motor skills: Specific dates again are unknown, but he was able to walk by 15 months, rode a tricycle early, and currently is able to ride a bicycle with training wheels.

Fine motor skills: It is reported that he is right-hand dominant, has not yet mastered coloring within the lines, but mastered zippers. He is able to write his name without difficulty, although this is somewhat messy.

Academic history: Currently, he attends nursery school, where academically he does well, but has significant behavior problems. For example, when Mom needed to have him off Tenex for approximately 1 week, the nursery school said that if he does not go back on medication, he will not be able to attend nursery school.

Major Illness: He did suffer from Giardia and also H. pylori, and received antibiotics for these, with resolution. He has always had difficulty with weight gain. Current medications include Tenex, along with multivitamin, cod liver oil, and L-Thionine.

Review of Systems: Review of systems does reveal history of innocent murmur, significant diarrhea with failure to thrive. Bone age was completed which was reported to be within 8 months of chronological age, although this is accurate only up to 6 months. It is reported that he does have low tone and mood swings. All other systems are reviewed and are negative.

Physical Examination: General observations: Richard was quite cooperative throughout the evaluation. He followed simple directions without difficulty, and was quite compliant. He did play with toys in the exam room, and did not seem to move from toy to toy. His height today is 99 cm, with a weight of 13.4 kg. Head circumference measured 18 1/2 inches, which made all of the above fall below the 3rd percentile. Facial features were dysmorphic with close-set eyes, flat bridge of nose, flat mid face, micrognatia, small upturned nose, all consistent with Fetal Alcohol Spectrum

Disorder. Skull was microcephalic. Spine was straight, muscle bulk and tone were low but within normal limits. He did show excavatum of the chest, along with hyperflexibility in joints.

Diagnosis/Impression: This is a young male who does have significant history of oppositional behaviors, along with mood swings, behavioral problems, and ADHD. Using facial photograph analysis, and the University of Washington Diagnostic Coding, Richard does show moderate facial features consistent with Fetal Alcohol Spectrum Disorder, along with growth below the 3rd percentile, and head circumference below the 3rd percentile, giving him a Diagnostic Clinical Summary Score which does show sentinel physical findings, along with static encephalopathy, all consistent with FASD.

Recommendations: At this time, we do recommend continuing psychological services, and also continuing nursery school. We have recommended social skill play, starting with one-to-one ratio in supervised setting, to assist with behaviors. We have also recommended initiating Risperdal 0.5 mg in a once daily dosing.

Lengthy discussion was held with his adoptive mother regarding condition and management, along with prognosis. The above diagnosis does place Richard at risk for learning disabilities, ADHD, and behavioral problems.

Fairy Tale Part 4: Chaos

The damage to his mind was terrible. Try as he might, Ricky couldn't stay out of trouble. Trouble, trouble, and more trouble! He just couldn't behave! It was too hard for him to learn from his mistakes because of his damaged brain, and his whole family was in chaos because of his wild behavior. What would become of this boy?

Stealing

Hey there again, Blogosphere. Sorry I come complaining to you all the time, but I have to vent to someone. I'm glad you're here. Even if no one ever reads this, it's good to write it. There was a minor stealing episode today, nothing out of the ordinary, but it stresses me out. Let me explain Ricky's stealing habit.

At first glance, anyone meeting Ricky would have trouble believing what I'm about to tell you. They call FAS an invisible disability for a reason. He looks like a nice, cute, all-American boy. Big smile, blonde hair, baseball cap turned sideways... But his disability isn't invisible to those of us who know him well. His behavior at home during 1st and 2nd grade was horrible. He was stealing and destroying things weekly. He stole my computer boot disks, notebooks, cellphones, chargers, digital cameras, and my husband's laptop, to name a few. These items were recovered. He also stole a neighbor's Blackberry, Alex's video system, books, papers, clothing, and even his very own toys. I'm sure he stole other things that were not recovered. He'd come home with things from school that I'd know weren't his. He'd always say his friends "gave" him stuff. I doubt it. Some things he stole would get hoarded away somewhere, while others would get picked to shreds with his hands, destroyed completely. I have no idea how he accomplished the destruction without tools, but he did.

No one in the house felt safe. Alex was locking all his important belongings in my room. Hazel wouldn't allow anyone in her room. I had to bring my purse to the bathroom with me, for fear of getting ripped off in my own home. We stopped visiting friends' houses because Ricky always managed to steal something, no matter how vigilantly we watched him. As you might imagine, the family was falling apart around his stealing. He couldn't be left unsupervised for 30 seconds. There were no consequences that mattered to him. He continued to steal.

One particularly crazy episode was the night he destroyed his own PSP (portable video game system), his most prized possession. (Yes, he even stole from himself!) He was in bed after a day with no major behavior problems. A successful day. He pretended to sleep when I checked him around 8:00. Then he snuck out of bed to get the PSP game, and hid under his covers with it. He took that metal object apart piece by piece, cutting his hands in the process, and then hid the broken game on his headboard shelf, under his Yankees cap. When I checked him again at 10:30 before going to bed, I found him asleep in what looked like a crime scene with blood all over his sheets.

Hundred Dollar School Day

——— Original Message ———

From: Mrs. Kelly
To: Margot
Subject: Ricky
Date: Wednesday

Hi,

I had to clean out your son's desk today, it was a disaster, and found a $100.00 shopping card that belonged to another student's family. The office had been frantic looking for it over a month ago. In fact, when the principal came into our classroom looking for it, Ricky spearheaded the search with him. I know the card meant nothing to your son, I'm sure he had no idea what it was, but there it was. I'm not sure if he took it out of another child's cubby or if it was placed in his accidentally.

I did not put it there, someone in the office did. So, this could be an accident.

Your son's behavior in school isn't dangerous, just disruptive. I do keep a close eye on him. He is rather difficult.

Keep in touch if there is anything I need to know.

Mrs. Kelly

———— Original Message ————

From: Margot
To: Mrs. Kelly
Subject: Re: Ricky
Date: Wednesday

Dear Mrs. Kelly,

I am sorry about the gift card. It was not an accident. After receiving your email, I asked him about the card in his desk. First he denied having it there. Then he said it appeared there, then he said he found it on the floor, then he said it fell out of a cubby, then he said it fell out of Matthew's cubby and landed in his desk, then he finally admitted taking it from Matthew's cubby and placing it in his desk. He is not in the least remorseful. Rather, he's annoyed at all the commotion about a card he doesn't care about. He said he will give it back, he "doesn't need it." I don't even know what to say.

He is in the habit of taking things that he knows are valuable to others and hiding them, although these things bring him no benefit nor joy once he has obtained them (recent examples: my computer disks and our neighbor's Blackberry, which he took while we were invited dinner guests). Also, he comes home often with little interesting doo-dads that are not his. He says his friends give him things, like pens, pencils, erasers, keychains, drawings with other kids' names on them, action figures, small toys, food, etc. This has been going on for years, and I am certain he steals them, I can tell by his face when I ask, but since I cannot investigate every pencil and eraser, I ignore…

I've been thinking over our discussion last week about your recommendation to explore alternative education options for Ricky. If you think he would benefit by being "out of district" in a therapeutic school (I think that's what they are called), please state that in your letter to the county. I don't want you to say it if you don't think it would be appropriate, but that is what I am going to push for once he is in public school. I feel that he is less learning disabled and more emotionally disturbed, but what do I know about these things?

Thanks again for all your kind attention to my son, and I'm sorry for the trouble he causes.

Best regards,
Margot

Mara Kendahl

——— Original Message ———

From: Mrs. Kelly
To: Margot
Subject: Re: Ricky
Date: Thursday

Hi,

Thank you for taking my call yesterday and further explaining the situation. Please don't apologize. Your son is not in trouble. His brain has been damaged, through no fault of his. It is just the way it is, and it is heartbreaking. I will give this plenty of thought and let you know, I think there is a wonderful school in Highland Park that deals with children with emotional disorders. The state of NJ does not recognize an ED classification any more. I don't know why. Check out Highland Park and see what you come up with.

    Good luck, this is just a sad situation all around. I will compose a letter by next week.

——— Original Message ———

From: Margot
To: Mrs. Kelly
Subject: Re: Ricky
Date: Friday

Thanks for your understanding, Mrs. Kelly. I will be keeping my son home from school today as requested by the principal.

My son likes school, and while I don't think this punishment will make a difference, because he does not understand cause and effect at all, I have to go through the motions of showing him consequences.

I know he is giving you a lot of extra work, but if it's not too much trouble, would you put some of this in writing for me? -- at your convenience, of course. Maybe you could include some of the classroom behavior that is disruptive and driving the other children crazy, as well as this incident of taking the money. It may help me to get services for him next year. I am hoping to find a residential education solution for him in the next few years, and this kind of documentation from you may help.

Please monitor my son closely and remove him from all activity if you suspect he is losing control. He has been doing poorly at home lately, and I feel he may be dangerous in loosely supervised situations. For example, he kicked his sister's (permanent) tooth out last week. I'm sorry you have to deal with this, too.

Best regards,
Margot

Sheets To The Wind

Hello?
[---]
Hey Mom, how's everything?
[---]
Good, good! Tell Aunt Mary I say hi when she gets there.
[---]
Oh, I'm all right. Been a long couple of days. I'm tired, and Ricky's just getting weirder and weirder.
[---]
Me, too.
[---]
Yeah, but every time anything happens, which is all the time, he just wants to change his medication. It never does any good.
[---]
One thing after another, but last night was really odd. You know how he gets up at night and does all sorts of nonsense right?

[---]

Well, last night I heard some rummaging around in the boys' room, but I didn't get up, I was exhausted. I laid in bed for a while, listening hard, then I got up to check if everything was OK. I tiptoed in like I always do, and Alex was asleep, but Ricky must have heard me because he was awake in his bed, face up, doing that thing he always does when he's awake but wants me to think he's sleeping. He's got his eyes closed up tight and his whole face squinted up and he's holding the covers up to his neck with his fists. So I didn't think there was a problem. He always does that. But this time he had piled mounds of blankets on his bed, but no big deal, right? No harm in that. So at breakfast I asked him what was with all the blankets, and he said he was cold. OK. So later I'm cleaning and doing laundry and stripping beds, and when I get to Ricky's bed, no sheets.

[---]

There were no sheets. Nothing but the blankets he'd piled there himself. The sheets had disappeared, along with the pillow and the bedspread. I was looking at a bare mattress.

[---]

I know. I looked around the room, under the beds, in the closet, in his drawers. There was a bad pee smell again in his drawers. I wish he'd stop peeing on his clean clothes. Then I checked the bathroom and the laundry room. No sheets.

[---]

Right? So I figured I'd have to wait for him to get home to tell me where he might've stashed them. On my way to pick the kids up from school, something, I don't know what, made me turn around and look back at the house. And I saw just a tiny spot of blue behind the front bushes under the boys' window. So I stopped the car and got out and guess what it was.

[---]

You are correct. In the front yard. In a pile behind a bush.

[---]

I know, wait. I'm getting to that. After school, I asked and showed him the bare bed. He said he didn't know, but I could tell by his face that he knew exactly what happened. So we go back and forth and then he says he threw the sheets out the window.

[---]

That's what I thought. The windows are so high up. How would he do it, right? Guess what. He did it. Here's what he did. He said he felt too tired to get up and pee, so he decided to pee the bed. Then he felt cold and wet, and decided he wasn't too tired anymore.

[---]

No, he told me this himself.

[---]

Right. So the sheets were in the yard behind the bushes all day.

[---]

How should I know what he was up to last night when I heard him rummaging around in there? I knew he wasn't sleeping, he was definitely awake, doing that face up, squinty, grinning, fake snoring thing. But I figured he'd just been roaming around like he always does.

[---]

I'd believe anything at this point. So anyway, he says he got up and stripped the bed and thought the best place for the sheets would be out the bathroom window. 'Cause that makes sense, right? So he opens that high bathroom window, climbed up on the toilet with all the sheets, and on tiptoe scooted those sheets, and the pillow, and the bedspread out the window. Then he went back to bed. That must be when he decided it was cold and went to get all those blankets.

[---]

I couldn't believe it either, but he did.

[---]

Damn right he could've fallen out the window!

[---]

I think he's too short and probably too weak to pull himself all the way up on the window. He would've had to've been on tiptoe with arms stretched to get those sheets out that window. I don't exactly understand how he did it.

[---]

Handled. The contractor is coming tomorrow to put safety bars on all the windows.

[---]

I asked him. I said, "Wouldn't throwing them on the floor have been a viable option?" "I didn't think of that," he said.

[---]

He didn't have one.

[---]

Oh my God is right. So we go out in the snow and bring the sheets in and put them in the laundry, which got him really pissed off and crazy, because you know how he doesn't like to touch anything. He felt like the sheets were dirty because they were out in the front yard. I had to take his arms and make him pick them up.

[---]

Because that psychologist the state sends, Michelle, she says consequences have to be real. If you dirty something, you clean it. If you break something, you fix it, etcetera. So I guess if you throw stuff out the window, you have to go in the yard and get it and put it in the laundry.

[---]

I dunno. I'm trying here.

[---]

I agree. But when he increases the medication, he ends up a drugged-out little zombie. That's not fair either. But I guess it's a discussion that has to be had. His new clothes are rags, the hole I told you about that he's scratching in the wall by his bed? It keeps getting bigger, and it's got blood on it, and he's going to lose one of his fingernails now.

[---]

Yeah, I know. I'm not sure what to do either.

Itchy

It's cold and I don't like when it's cold. So many clothes. They itch. Mom says if I don't think about it they won't itch but they do itch. It feels good to scratch when it itches. I like to scratch. My nails need to grow longer. I don't want to wait but if they would grow longer I could scratch better. I don't like going to bed early either but Mom's mad again so I have to go to bed. Mom said to go to sleep but I don't know how so it's not really my fault if I'm awake. She says if I lay still and close my eyes I will sleep but I know that's a lie. If I lay still with my eyes closed I don't really lay still because sometimes I'll feel itchy and sometimes I have to pee and other times I can feel my eyes moving under my eyelids so I know I'm not really lying still and if I don't lay still I won't sleep. But it's not early anymore because now Alex came to bed and he didn't have to go to bed early so maybe it's regular bed time. And now I can hear him breathing so I think he's asleep but sometimes I like to check if he's asleep really or if he's faking like I fake when Mom checks if I'm sleeping. Alex doesn't really lay still

Mara Kendahl

like Mom says because he breathes loud and that makes the lump of him under his covers go up and down and that's not still. Also he makes loud breathing not like regular breathing where you can't really hear it. If I tiptoe to his bed and put my head on him I feel him going up and down and sometimes if I pull the covers off him I can hear his heart making thumping sounds and sometimes he swats at me and makes grumpy noises and then I run to jump back in my bed and then Mom comes in and I fake and she covers Alex and then stands over my bed for a long time. Then she kisses me and I think she can never know that I'm faking sleep and I smile because I'm happy that she doesn't know. I make sure I do loud breathing like Alex especially when she stands over the bed.

Sometimes when I have to pee the bathroom is too far and too loud and I like to pee in the shirt drawer because it's cool the way I can pee there and it doesn't make any noise and the pee soaks straight into the shirts and disappears. It's like a secret. Mom gets mad and says everything smells like pee but if the pee disappears as soon as it drops onto the shirts then it's not really pee anymore because the pee never made any noise and then it's not really there if you can't see it either. In the morning the nice lines and dots I made on the shirts is gone so there's no more pee. The night after Grandma and Grandpa came over for dinner I went to bed early because Mom said I was misbehaving but really I wasn't everyone else was but I was the one who got sent to bed in my feety pajamas the ones I like so I pick holes in them with my fingers because I like them but if I have to scratch I need to get my fingers in so with holes they're better. Mom wants to throw them out because she said I ruined them with picking but I like them better now. I was in my bed and I thought if I pee the bed the pee should disappear just like it does in the shirt drawer but it didn't. Mom doesn't like it when I wake her at night but I didn't because I knew what to do. Mom takes the sheets off the bed so I did the same thing because the sheets felt warm first but changed to cold and smelly too. So when something is smelly it's supposed to be in the bathroom, that's what Mom said, when I poo it has to be in the bathroom because that's where you make smelly stuff. But there was no room in the bathroom for all the sheets, so I put them out the window to make room. It was better in bed without the sheet but my pajamas were still cold. I got new ones and put the old ones back in the drawer. If I put them on the floor Mom doesn't like a mess of clothes on the floor or especially crumbs from the wall shouldn't be on the floor. Mom says I put the wall crumbs on the floor but the crumbs from the wall fall all by themselves. Sometimes when I'm itchy I scratch the wall so maybe the whole room won't be so itchy anymore. Then little dusty pieces fall out but it's not me that makes the pieces it's the wall. And the wall keeps making a bigger and bigger hole and the hole is filled with itchy dust so when I scratch the dust comes out and it's better. Sometimes though it's not so nice because my fingernail bleeds and Mom gets mad when I bleed but I told her the wall did it I didn't do it. She's always mad at stuff I didn't do and then I have to talk to Michelle about it with curly hair at the kitchen table. I don't like to talk to Michelle because her games aren't fun and she talks quiet and then I talk quiet and then she tells me to speak up.

County Team

County Special Education Services Commission
Union County Division
1st Grade, Our Lady of Mercy School

Student preferred name: Ricky

Richard was referred to the Child Study Team for evaluation because of his attentional and learning difficulties. In addition, he has exhibited oppositional and defiant behavior, difficulty in transitioning between activities, and difficulty in social interactions with peers. He has suffered medical problems as well, including gastrointestinal and feeding issues, "significant" failure to thrive, and possible allergies. He has been evaluated by a number of professionals.

    Richard's overall health is good at this time and he is sleeping well. He goes to bed about 7 p.m. and this provides him with approximately an hour of active home time after he returns home from his after school program. His appetite varies with the effectiveness of his medications and he remains small for his age.

Richard does not seem to exhibit a wide range of emotions, but changes between relative contentedness and feeling upset when he is on a relatively "even keel," and between hyperactive and angry modes when he is not. He realizes when he has done something unacceptable or wrong. Richard also still exhibits a high pain tolerance. When he was in Puerto Rico this past summer, he was able to "hold it together" behaviorally for a while, but then became extremely trying for his caretaker to manage.

Richard cannot occupy himself without outside direction and will wander about aimlessly if left on his own. He will watch television for about 15 minutes at a time and then will wander off. He enjoys playing with his Nintendo video game device and will become upset if it is taken away as a punishment, but he seems to then quickly forget about having owned it. He will build a specific block project if asked and will focus on it, but will not produce much if left to the blocks on his own.

His teacher views Ricky as a charming, delightful child, though hard to handle. She sees Ricky's wanting to succeed and his eagerness to please his teachers as his greatest strengths. She notes that Ricky is proud on the occasions that he produces quality work. He is a strong reader.

No More Running Around

Hi! What's going on, Mom?
[---]
Sounds like a full day. Who's taking you, Aunt Mary or Dad?
[---]
Good plan, that'll be fun. How about you all come over for dinner after?
[---]
Oh. Ok. Well, another time.
[---]
He's ok. Well, not really. We got some bad news about the track team yesterday.
[---]
Yeah, how'd you know? Of course they kicked him off. We were hoping that track would give him a chance. I mean, point the kid in the right direction and tell him to run, right?
[---]

I'm sorry too, and I feel so stupid. I had these visions of him running track meets and feeling great about himself. He needs to have some successes sometimes, for chrissake. But it's not gonna happen. I mean, the first practice went well, and I was envisioning years of sitting on bleachers at track and field events, and wearing the school colors, and Ricky so proud of himself. But by the third week of practice, I received a note home from the coach. Ricky is misbehaving during practice. Not listening. Raging around hitting the other kids on the head with the relay batons. I begged them to keep him.

[---]

Of course I talked to him. He thought the track team was awesome. He really *wanted* to behave so he could stay on the team. By the fourth week they were politely asking me not to send him back. They didn't kick him off, exactly. But they made it clear that while he was God's little angel, he was a disruption and not exactly an asset to the team, and they asked me to return him to aftercare for his after school activities, instead of the track team.

[---]

Of course he is. He's devastated. He has absolutely no understanding that he brought this on himself.

[---]

Yeah, ok. Have a great time. Maybe you guys want to come over for dinner?

[---]

I did? Oh, right. Maybe another time.

In Pencil

*H*ey Blogosphere, how's everything? Tonight, I wish I could write this post in pencil instead of on a laptop keyboard. It would be so apropos…

I'm in bed with the laptop, ready to write this post, when I looked over at my nightstand and realized the pencil I leave tied there (in case I wake up in the middle of the night and need to write something down) is gone, which means Ricky took it, and maybe ate it. I kid you not.

One day last month when Ricky was having a typical bad day, sort of like today, talking back like crazy, in a terrible mood all afternoon, shrieking, carrying on, throwing himself around, dinner strewn on the kitchen floor, temper tantrums, food in his hair, etc. ugh, it never ends…

Anyway, that day last month that I started talking about, we sent him outside to jump on the trampoline for a while. That usually worked a little to calm him (and everyone else) down. When he came in, Bert gave him a book called "50 Things a Young Gentleman Should Know" to read aloud. He was reading a passage about why it is not nice to pass gas in front of others. They read the chapter together. They talked about it. Bert asked Ricky questions and he answered them perfectly appropriately. Hugs and high-fives all around. Then Ricky walked into the room where Hazel and I were sitting, and with  effort, let one rip. Then he couldn't understand why we didn't think it was awesome, and he stormed away.

I checked up on him about a half hour later. He was in his bed, and his quilt was soaking wet in a couple different places. He insisted he had no idea why. C'mon. So finally he admitted he was spitting on the quilt. (We had an episode over the weekend where he spit all over his bedroom floor, making quite a puddle for his older brother to step in.) I asked him why he spit. He said he didn't. I asked him why he lied about the spitting. He said he didn't.

I asked, "Did you spit on the quilt and then tell me you don't know how the quilt got wet?"

"Yes."

"So you spit and then lied about spitting."

"No."

I thought my head might explode. I shouldn't engage the conversation, but Michelle (his psychologist) says I have to give him a chance to work out his thoughts, explain himself, and come clean. But all that nonsense aside, who purposely soils where they sleep? Then I found something gross on his headboard shelf–wet, chewed, pencils with the pencil stalk

Mara Kendahl

eaten off up to the eraser. Sort of like a cigarette smoked down to the filter. He admitted matter-of-fact that he ate them. The spitting he has done before, and it's crazy–but eating pencils? Who does that? I remember Dr. Patel told me once he might eventually eat things that aren't food, but I wasn't sure what that meant. Now I know. I wonder what else he's eating. I don't want to know. But like I said, my pencil is gone.

Dear Parents

Dear Parents,

Ricky went into the red zone (extreme misbehavior) during gym class. Mr. G gave him numerous warnings and had to give him a time-out. During time out, Ricky continued to misbehave. Mr. G informed me that Ricky refused to follow directions. Please discuss this at home tonight with your son.

Blessings,
Mr. C
Principal
Our Lady of Mercy School

• • •

Dear Parents,

Due to inappropriate behavior, your child Ricky has entered the extreme danger zone on our chart. When a child reaches this point, a note is sent home to notify the parents. Ricky hit three other children during recess. A kindergarten child, a 1st grader and a 2nd grader. Ricky had no reason nor explanation for why he did this. I anticipate better behavior in the future and look forward to Ricky having more success regarding classroom behavior. Thank you for your support in this matter.

Blessings,
Mr. C
Principal
Our Lady of Mercy School

• • •

Dear Parents,
...

• • •

Dear Parents,
...

• • •

Dear Parents,
...

Chapter 5
A Fairy Tale: Disruption

*H*is new mommy's heart ached. Hoping to help Ricky, she sent him to live with her cousin in the jungle, where he might run free, learn a trade, and build his future. But that cousin couldn't handle him, and she sent him home. Ricky returned to his local school where he continued to disrupt and cause trouble.

Try Something New

Hey again, Blogosphere. I thought Ricky's school was all squared away this year, but unfortunately, things have not been going as planned. And he was so happy. Such a shame. The poor kid. He's in 3rd grade, and he's been in 4 different schools.

School is a challenge for him. His capacity to learn, behave, and focus is pretty limited. Sometimes, he just gets up and wanders off when he is expected to sit and listen, or study, or participate in an activity, etc. Also, there are some concepts he just can't get. His brain damage affects the frontal lobe, which processes cause-and-effect, decision making and judgment, impulse control, and abstract concepts such as time and money. Sometimes I think it's the "common sense" section of the brain, but what do I know?

Ricky struggled through nursery school. I had him evaluated by the public school system for special education, and they told me there was nothing wrong with him, and he did not need special ed. I disagreed. I went to the SPAN NJ

(State Parent Advocacy Network of New Jersey) and was told that my town was one of the most litigious in the state, and my son would likely never get what he needs, and that I would spend huge sums on long drawn out court battles. The SPAN representative suggested I move to a neighboring town. Ridiculous.

Private School: We sent Ricky to an expensive kindergarten in an upscale town. He struggled with his behavior and with the academic material. The teacher, an angel from heaven (actually Korea) named Miss Heather, kept him for 1/2 hour every day to work with him alone on academics. She was a Godsend. That made all the difference, and he eventually improved academically and even learned to read, something Patel said wouldn't be likely to happen. But that school was just for kindergarten. There was no first grade option. Meanwhile, his behavior at home became more challenging.

(Ricky spent the summer between kindergarten and first grade with his aunt in Puerto Rico. We all needed a break. He enjoyed himself, and it was a successful summer for all.)

Catholic School: First grade at Our Lady of Mercy had about 13 kids in the class, while the public school had 23. I opted for the nurturing environment the Catholic school promised, and the smaller class size. Also, the first grade teacher was reputed to be a saint. She was. Ricky did all right academically with the teacher's special attention but was having behavior issues right off the bat. By end of September he was pulled out for testing and it was determined that he needed extra help. A week later, the County Department of Education Child Services Team was there to evaluate him. Surprise! They classified him immediately. You see, the Catholic schools do not take money out of their own budgets to provide services to classified kids, the county foots the bill, so the school (and especially the teacher) clamors to get the kid classified so they can bring in help. The public schools, on the other hand, have to pay for special ed services from their already-established budgets, so the special ed kids are considered a drain on funding. The public schools would often rather fight you (they have lawyers on staff) than provide services. Financially, it makes sense. Morally and ethically, it stinks.

Ricky was classified by the County Team as OHI by December (Other Health Impaired, which means there's a problem, but they don't know how to classify it). His tests completely baffled the child study team, who had between them been working with the county special ed team for about 100 years. They said he was so strong in some areas and so totally lacking in others that some tests couldn't even be scored properly.

By the end of first grade, Ricky was stealing and lying pretty regularly. The school had had enough of him. The teacher and principal suggested at the end of the year (in writing) that the school was not equipped to handle his needs and that we should try public school.

(Ricky spent the summer between first and second grade in Puerto Rico again. An almost-successful summer with only a few stealing episodes; though, I suspect much of his petty theft went unnoticed and/or unreported.)

Public School: Second grade in public school was awful. He had a mediocre teacher. No specific complaints about her, she was just coasting her way through on tenure, waiting for summer vacation and ultimately retirement. Ricky's classification followed him, so he entered 2nd grade classified OHI, was given a minimal assistance, and was not given an aide. Some examples of how well the school watched a disabled kid: He did not do homework for weeks, and I was not notified. (He would destroy the homework before coming home, so I didn't know it existed.) He didn't eat lunch for months before a classmate of Ricky's called it to my attention. He stole small items from his classroom and peers almost daily, but went unnoticed. He didn't understand the academic material, and his grades were awful. It was a disaster. His behavior became strange and unmanageable at home as well. His stealing habit had become overwhelming. Seriously, it was like living with a poltergeist. Bert and I were barely coping with him. The kids were angry. Our marriage was deteriorating. So we decided to try something new for 3rd grade, and it was working. Until this weekend. Which is what I wanted to write about tonight, but now I'm beat. More tomorrow.

Show Me The Money

———— Original Message ————

From: Director Reyes
To: Margot
Subject: medical care for your son in PR

Hi. It was my pleasure to discuss the care needs of your son last week. I just found out the information for your son. For Lares, the children with special needs their services are in Centro Pediatrico route 129 in Arecibo. Is located in the grounds of the Arecibo Regional Hospital. They have a pediatric doctor Dr. Arzola, whose specialty is neurodevelopment. Also Dr. Marisa Cruz a pediatrician. The payment will depend on the insurance. The best is to call and get the information. Hopefully this will help. Please let me know if you receive the email. Maria

• • •

Maria N. Reyes Medina, MSW
Directora Asociada/Associate Director
Instituto de Deficiencias en el Desarrollo/Developmental Deficiencies Institute
Escuela Graduada de Salud Publica/Graduate School of Public Health
Universidad de Puerto Rico/University of Puerto Rico
Recinto de Ciencias Medicas/Department of Medical Sciences

——— Original Message ———

From: Margot
To: Director Reyes
Subject: Re: medical care for your son in PR

Dear Director,

Thanks again for all your help. However, after speaking with the personnel at the Centro Pediatrico in Arecibo, I understand that the doctors there have no one on staff experienced with treating Fetal Alcohol Syndrome. Do you have anyone on staff at the Instituto de Deficiencias en el Desarrollo who works with and understands children with FAS, including prescribing medicines such as Risperdal, Intuniv, Abilify, and/or Concerta?
    Thank you in advance for your kind assistance.

Best regards,
Margot

——— Original Message ———

From: Director Reyes
To: Margot
Subject: Re: medical care for your son in PR

Hi Margot. I consult your situation with Dr. Lelis Nazario a child psychiatrist at Hospital Pediatrico in Arecibo. She indicates that your first step is to have medical insurance. It can be a private insurance or state funded insurance (la reforma). They have a clinic for children at Hospital Pediatrico the name of the clinic is Clinica Pediatrica de Salud Mental de Nino y Adolescente. They accept private insurance and la reform, if they have Lares assigned as their catchment area. You call for an appointment and they will have him evaluated. I hope this can be helpful.

——— Original Message ———

From: Margot
To: Director Reyes
Subject: Re: medical care for your son in PR

As discussed at length last week on the phone, I am prepared to pay for my son's treatment, and we already have private insurance. However, I see how important the insurance aspect of care is, and I will look into procuring a local insurance plan again. Thank you, Doctor, for your help.

Best regards,
Margot

Summers

*H*ey Blogosphere, I was telling you in the last post about all the schools Ricky's been in, and here we are in third grade. Which isn't going so well. Understatement. Here was the plan. Ricky was supposed to attend 3rd grade in Puerto Rico. It was all set. And it was going well for a while. Now everything's been shot to hell. Let me take a step back and pick up where I left off.

My husband grew up in rural Puerto Rico and came to NJ with his family at 15 years old. We spend a week or two there every year since we met ten years ago. We always brought the children with us. We decided it was important for them to maintain ties with the island, as the children are 1/2 Hispanic growing up in a White neighborhood. It's good for the kids to see that unlike

in NJ, in Puerto Rico all the doctors, lawyers, bankers, business people, mayors, and even the governor, are all Puerto Rican!

We started spending one month every summer in Lares, a low-income, rural community in the western central part of the island. It's the type of community where the same families have been living for generations, no one locks doors, and children roam the neighborhoods freely, being fed at any house and being scolded by any adult.

The school year in PR starts early in August and ends mid-May. So Bert and I had an ingenious plan a few years ago. We enrolled all three kids in a private school for a month–books, uniforms, and all. We spent a month lounging, riding the Harley, and roaming the island by day, while the kids spent a month in "Spanish camp." They made friends, learned, and improved their Spanish language. It was great. We did this for 2 years before the older two kids figured out it was real school and revolted.

The first year the kids spent August attending L'Academia Cristiana de Lares, Ciudad del Rey, Ricky was in nursery school. There were 9 children in his class, and nursery school in PR consists of lots of running around outside. Under those circumstances, he almost held it together for a month, although the teacher asked me if he had ever been tested for learning disabilities. (I stifled a scream.) We were so happy with how the summer went for everyone that we bought a small bungalow in Lares and fixed it up, so we could stay in it every summer instead of renting. It was such a success for everyone, and we hadn't had lots of successes.

The following summer, the kids went back to school, and Ricky attended kindergarten. The director told me randomly, after no complaints all month, that the school was not equipped to handle him, and he might not be allowed to re-enroll the following summer. So here I thought everything was great, and it was just that they weren't telling me what was going on.

When the next summer came around, we sent Ricky down to PR early, in June, (it had been a long year, and he wanted to go) to stay with his Aunt Nidia for the summer, until we could meet up with him in August. The other two children didn't go to school that summer, but Ricky did a month of 1st grade. The school took him because we begged and promised it would only be a month, and that it would be the last time. (They are such good people at that school!) At the end of the month, they made it clear that 2nd grade would not be an option, and indeed that was the last summer they accepted him.

The following summer, we didn't have the nerve to ask L'Academia about a month of 2nd grade, but Ricky was dying to go to PR. (He asked every day starting January 1st, "How many days til PR?") We arranged for him to spend the whole summer with Aunt Nidia and attend an all-day local sports-and-recreation camp. It worked out great according to Ricky, but just barely ok according to camp staff.

So this past summer, the summer before 3rd grade, he went to PR two weeks before the rest of us. He was so happy to get out there and roam around outside and play with all the neighborhood animals. (Nidia had a scare with him, though, when he taunted a dog and the animal nipped him.) Then, once we got there, he had a couple incidents of stealing from neighbors, and an incident of fighting with his little cousin Leti, but nothing that couldn't be dealt with. Ricky would ask how many days until we had to go home, and then he'd cry.

We decided to let him attend 3rd grade all year in PR. Puerto Rico is a state (not a UNITED state, but a FREE ASSOCIATED state) and the schools are governed by US federal law. Just like in NJ. No child left behind, and all that. And we're residents, so why not? We thought that the small school in a nurturing community where he can play outside every day would be beneficial for him and his behavior. And it made him happy, which was key. The standards in the local schools didn't seem quite as rigorous as ours, so he might experience small successes, which he needs. Nidia was eager to host him all year, and my husband and I agreed to take turns flying down monthly for visits.

It took all summer, but we were able to put an IEP together with the school staff, principal, social worker, local medical professionals, school nurse, and a lawyer. And off he went to his new school! We were hoping he would spend a whole successful school year there. We thought trying something completely new, something he'd love, might work.

Baby Cousin

Today is the worst day and I hate everybody especially Mom and Dad and Leti. Everyone is so mean. I hate going to my room all because of stupid cousin Leti. She's only 6 she's such a baby. I hate when she tries to play with me because I don't want to play with her. All I was doing was digging in the dirt. Mom said I could dig in the dirt. She doesn't like it when I scratch the wall, but she said I could scratch the ground and take as much dirt and scratch as much as I want. I get to scratch my fingers in it and no one bothers me and no one tells me not to scratch but today Dad came mad and beat me with the belt and it's not fair. I told him Mom said I could dig but he kept hitting me because of Leti. She ruined everything. I don't even like her. I didn't ask her she just showed up in the yard and started talking blah blah blah about girl stuff blah blah and I didn't care because I was digging. Then she wanted to see what I was digging and she was running all around the nice hole I was making and I didn't want her there in the way but she started digging a little and I

Angel of Disruption

was so nice I let her stay because Mom says be nice. And when I walked to the fence to pee she followed me and I said to her why doesn't she pee too and she said girls don't pee outside and I said Mom told me to pee outside so I don't get the house dirty and now that she's digging with me she'll have to pee outside too or Mom will get mad. I said everyone has to follow the rules and anyway I'm the older cousin so if I say it she has to do it. She said ok and took her pants down to pee and she didn't even have a wiener! She had a cut like a sideways flap where her wiener should be and so I tried to reach in and pull that wiener out of there. But stupid Leti was slapping me and hiding her wiener inside that little flap and it was sticky like the inside of my nose. And I tried to scratch it out, her wiener, but she kept moving so I had to hold her down and she was slapping at me like the baby she is and she punched me with her baby hand and punching isn't nice and I punched her back because she started it. That's when she screamed real loud and I yelled at her to take her wiener out and she kept up that bad screeching and hiding her wiener inside and then Mom came running. Mom picked me up off Leti and said to stop fighting. And that's when stupid baby Leti started talking blah blah blah and crying waaa waaa and Mom listened to her and not me and made me go inside and it hurt my wrist how she was taking me and she put me in my room. And I asked can't I dig without Leti getting in the way and I told on Leti that she wouldn't pee at the fence but Mom said I had to stay in my room and all she cared about was stupid crying Leti. And Mom called Daddy to come home from Titi's and then she was crying too just like Leti and when Daddy came home he didn't listen to me and he beat me with the belt. And now

Mara Kendahl

Leti left and I'm glad she's gone and I hope she never comes back and I don't know why Mom's crying because no one beat *her* with the belt.

It Really Could Have

Sorry I ended my last post so abruptly, Blogosphere. A minor emergency, but nothing out of the ordinary.

Back to spending 3rd grade in PR: It could have worked. Besides some defiant behavior, he was doing well in the school, earning good grades and making a friend or two. Nidia is the one who couldn't handle him. In fairness, she was going through some personal issues at the time, and adding Ricky to her life was not working. She wanted him, wanted to keep him for the year, and counted on the monthly check we sent. However, in my estimation, she was overwhelmed and not handling his situation properly.

I hate it that he can't finish out the year in PR. Hate it! But I have to go with my gut and get him out of her house. I'm so mad at Nidia! And I'm so sad that Ricky won't have this opportunity. He even made the "A Team" in the town's baseball league! Making "A" in PR is a big deal, because the kids play baseball all year round, and most are extremely accomplished players, even in the third grade. In NJ, he can't play baseball again until spring. He loves baseball. School was going fine… It's only October….

His aunt blew it, but again, I'm too tired to tell the rest right now. Sorry to keep you hanging, Blogosphere. Thanks for being a patient friend. Goodnight.

Stolen

Hi again Blogosphere, I hope your day was better than Ricky's. He came home from school confused, as he tends to do more and more often as he gets older. He doesn't understand why the teachers yell at him and why his "friends" don't like him. He's starting to understand his differences and limitations. He's hurt and frustrated, and it's heartbreaking.

That woman who drank while she was pregnant with him, I won't dignify her with the title "mother" because she is everything a real mother isn't. That woman robbed a poor innocent angel when she drank. She damaged him forever, stole everything from him.

She stole his childhood. He should have been in friends' houses playing with blocks and cars and legos. Instead, he's been at doctors and therapies, playing those things in offices with health care workers.

She stole his friends. Most of his peers find him hard to like. But he has so much goodness inside him. He's so much

Mara Kendahl

more than just a bundle of bad behaviors. He likes jazz, and sings along so sweetly. Multicolored salads make him happy, and he asks for cauliflower and sunflower seeds like a kid at an ice cream store asks for sprinkles and hot fudge. He's great at basketball, and shoots like a pro. And he loves small animals and insects and, when the meds are right and he's capable, cares for them with tenderness. Why should he grow up isolated? He's got a beautiful little soul inside of him. He doesn't mean to act out.

She stole his high school diploma and his pride in earning it. I hope he can get through high school, but chances are... ugh, I can't even think about it.

She stole his career. Who knows what he could have been? He'll be lucky if he can live independently and hold down a job. But he's so smart! It's not fair! He could have been anything he wanted to be. Maybe, he would have been someone great. Now, the world will never know. We all lost something.

She stole his wife and kids. Had he been born healthy, he might have had a beautiful wife who adored him, children to raise and be proud of, and grandchildren to brighten his old age. The woman who might have married him–what direction will her life take now? It's unlikely that his children and grandchildren will ever be born.

People who abuse and damage babies are criminals and belong in jail. That woman, that child abuser, that criminal who damaged my son and stole everything from him, his friends and family, his accomplishments and career, his pride and future–she got away with it.

Blood Oranges

Nidia scuff-tapped in bedazzled flip-flops from her sweaty unmade bed. It was early, and hot, a perfect day to stay away from the orange factory. No more peeling oranges. Just babysitting. *Gracias, Papà Dios, for this job.* She peeked in the doorway across from hers and found Ricky asleep, damp, his blond hair moist on his forehead, his white-round face cherubic. Only his face was round, she noted not for the first time. Such a handsome face. *He's mental, but you'd never know it by looking at that little face, tan chulo, so cute.* The rest of his body was wiry-skinny and stunted, not quite right for a nine-year-old. *It's easy to like him when he's sleeping.*

Stepping out of the flip-flops, she tiptoed quietly into his room and started searching. Stashed under his bed she found a CD, her hairbrush, and her portable alarm clock. In his bedside table she found a can opener barely hidden under a pair of worn underwear. Scolding him was useless. Every day he squirreled something away. Others called it stealing, but she didn't mind retrieving her belongings; he never went far with them. After a week, she expected the petty theft, and the morning search had become routine. Still, she slept with her pocketbook, just in case.

She gave small tugs to the front of her flimsy night shirt to create puffs of air against her skin and slipped her flip-flops back on. From the hallway, she tossed the CD and the clock onto her bed. As she scuff-tapped past the bathroom, she flipped the brush into the sink. Can opener in hand, she passed her own son's 8th grade graduation photo and the portrait of Jesus en route to the kitchen of the squat, cement, 4-room house.

Waffles. The boy likes waffles. Nidia reached behind the floral curtain duct taped to the underside of the kitchen sink to retrieve the heavy, ancient waffle iron and held it against her body with one strong arm while she cleared space on the cluttered counter with her free hand. The open cubby next to the refrigerator held her dented tin bowl, whisk, and ingredients for the waffles. She cracked two of her neighbor's chickens' eggs into the bowl, then smelled the milk suspiciously before adding it, too. The table's one short leg clack-clacked while she whisked.

Barking outside. *Stop rushing me*, she muttered. Tyson growled for food and water under the searing tropical sun, pulling at his chain, making metallic scrambling-jingling sounds on the gravel driveway. Tyson was feared in this rural, hilly *barrio*, and wasn't allowed off his chain. Nidia, fancying herself as young and beautiful as she was a decade ago, believed the watchdog, a gift from an ex-boyfriend, was a testament to her beauty, which in truth hadn't been grand and had since faded.

The whisking and proximity to the heated waffle iron produced more dampness on her skin and brow. Nidia poured the batter, set the timer, and clamped the top before heading outside.

The garden hose was strewn in the front lawn where the boy had left it yesterday. He hadn't rolled and stowed it next to the washing machine as asked. She bent to pick it up, creaking and popping at the knees, and filled Tyson's grimy water dish.

Surveying the grounds, she decided to tidy the property. The tiny, flat-roofed house sat on a large piece of unkempt land at the end of a long gravel road. Caribbean jungle had grown up on all sides. Only the front was cleared, with a small yard that used to be paved, but had given way to insistent grasses and weeds. Strewn about were old car parts her ex had left, empty containers of white paint, a bleach bottle and a few beer cans, some piles of sand and cinder blocks, and various broken clothespins. She pinched the edge of a crumpled beer can between two brightly manicured fingers and released it. *It's too hot to clean today. Mañana.*

She checked that the duck's feeder was still out of Tyson's reach, and bent to pet the mangy Snoopy, a matted little filthy-white street mutt she called hers who had come running to greet her, knotty tail wagging furiously. Hopping and wagging still, he followed her to the washing machine on the front porch. She had washed the boy's sheets the night before, and they needed to be hung. Yesterday, after dinner, she noticed a bitter urine smell by the boy's bed. She was certain she hadn't smelled it earlier on her morning rounds. She suspected he stood bedside and peed the bed purposely, but when asked, he denied it with a "tsk" and a shake of his head. *It's hard to keep up with the boy's messes.* A thwack to the clothesline that ran to the coconut tree sent a lizard flying. Happy Snoopy laid by in the shade, keeping Nidia quiet company until she finished her chore, then followed her, tail wagging, hoping to be invited inside.

At the screen door Nidia looked through the messy living room chock-a-block with trinkets on every flat surface, into the shabby kitchen. The boy was seated at the rickety table, picking intently at his fingers, his pink face sleepy and flushed with the heat. Nidia patted Snoopy before leaving him outside. When the boy heard the screen door slam behind Nidia, he nervously sat on his hands. He'd been warned not to pick at his fingers. Unchecked, he'd pick quietly until he bled.

"*Buenos dias, Titi,*" he said flatly. He was in his favorite grey shirt, the one with holes that he had bitten and poked himself. He waited, still sitting on his hands, until Nidia set his waffles down before him between the water-filled soda bottles meant to shoo flies. He picked up his fork and stabbed a waffle hard, then pushed the plate away and asked for eggs. Before she could reply, he slid from his chair, took two running steps, and launched himself onto the livingroom couch.

The boy's damp skin stuck to the faded cushion's plastic slip cover; his mouth hung slack as he stared at the blinking-binging video game on the portable color TV. He concentrated, volume blaring, while Nidia ate her waffles standing at the sink. After cleaning and storing the waffle iron, she realized the timer was gone from the counter. *I don't need it right now.* She scuff-tapped to the small bathroom whose door was visible from the livingroom to start her daily beauty routine. First a hair brush, next a hot straightening iron, then oversized curlers and a spray bottle filled with a homemade mixture of water and fragrance. Hair set, she applied lotion to fend off the inevitable wrinkles, then foundation, mascara, and eyeliner, all purchased on sale at Walmart. A touch of rouge, eyeshadow, and lipstick, also Walmart buys, and she was done. She examined herself in the mirror, almost satisfied. Chipped, multicolored nails tapped on the counter as she removed the curlers, one by one, and stowed her prized cosmetics in repurposed margarine containers. Every so often she poked her head out of the bathroom door to check on the boy.

"Titi, I want eggs!" He called when he saw her head.

She withdrew her head and instead stuck her arm out to point one long-nailed finger at the kitchen, where his waffles laid untouched and shrivelled on the table. She crossed the hall to her bedroom and took her time dressing.

A warm-sour odor. "*Huele!*" She called out, "*What smells!?*"

No reply.

"*Que huele?*"

Silence, followed by the slam of the screen door.

She poked her head out again. The acid-foul stink was stronger in the livingroom, and the boy was gone. *It's ok, there's nowhere to go but outside under the burning sun.* Nidia found the video game blinking on the screen, the controller on the floor, and the couch askew, with one side pulled out as though someone wanted to retrieve a fallen item.

Behind the couch lay a quiet turd, steaming, stinking. *Dios Mio!*

She went to the doorway and stood one hand on hip, held the screen open, and called his name. He came running, stopped with a jump just inches from the front porch, and pulled off one shoe. He always obeyed the no-shoes-inside rule. He had his second dusty shoe in his hand when Nidia asked, "Why did you do that?"

He looked up, startled. The blank stare of innocence.

"*Por que?*" she repeated.

He rolled his eyes up and to the left. Then, his pink mouth puckered in a tiny O and his eyes widened and met hers.

That's disgusting. Sucio! Why did you do that!? He stood still, staring. She felt her patience slipping again, already, her skin dampening under her arms and at the nape of her neck.

"No more video games for you today. You are punished."

"Can I have eggs, please, Titi?"

At her refusal, he put his shoes back on and marched away from the house, to nowhere.

Cleaning mierdas. This isn't what I expected. Nidia considered this nanny position a step up in life. Proud of her accomplishment, working for an important rich family from "over there," winning trust, earning a higher wage, and managing her own time from home, she gloated. She bragged to Yoli from the orange factory that she's practically her own boss: she can wake up when she wants, take breaks when she wants, and even watch TV and paint her nails while she's on the clock. Yoli felt pangs of jealousy, and told all the other girls at the factory of Nidia's unmerited luck and laziness. By the time the story blazed through the workers, Nidia was despised, a spoiled princess. One co-worker had asked for a small loan before Nidia had even received her first week's pay. *What a band of bochincheras y entrometi'as, gossipers and busybodies. They'll peel oranges all their lives. Not me. I'm going to make money, get out of here. I'll move to Camden with the money I save. Pay for my airfare and rent a studio apartment like my sister and her husband, ex-husband, did two years ago. There are jobs over there, good jobs for me, and even men with jobs! Papà Dios, please help me save enough money to move to Camden.* Nidia picked absently at a mosquito bite. *Retard Nanny…that's what my sister called me, but I'm a smart businesswoman.*

A squeaky shriek from outside. The boy often makes odd noises by himself, like the whoops he made eating a spider the other day. *I told him not to eat spiders, and the next day I caught him again with a disgusting spider in his hand.* The boy had stuck his tongue out as far as he could, looked her straight in the eye, and used two precise fingers to dangle the spider by one tiny leg. He wiped the spider across the length of his tongue and whooped. *Look, Titi,* he had said, *I don't eat the spider, I just lick him!* Nidia's stomach lurched at the memory.

Through the screen door she saw the boy's small bony back. He was sitting cross legged in the driveway facing the street, Snoopy in his arms. Snoopy's squirming was desperate; the boy must have been holding too tightly. With a twist of his skinny torso, backbone protruding, the boy moved Snoopy to the side and looked down at his lap, then threw his head back and shrieked again, one quick, shrill clap of a scream.

The screen door slammed. The boy turned to see Nidia approaching and released Snoopy, who bolted for the woods. When the boy stood, his pants remained in a pile on the ground. He was naked, his thighs awash in fresh blood. Red blood shining slick in the bright glare. Nidia felt the world slow down, the volume lower. Her vision narrowed onto his crotch – blood -- her peripheral vision dark, focused at the center – blood – there -- panic pounding loud in her ears.

Smeared. Red. All over the boy. He touched his privates and came away with two blood soaked hands. A snapshot before Nidia's eyes: his frail, bleeding body with two outstretched bloodied palms, eyebrows furrowed and head cocked to one side. She ran. She lifted him like a baby and rushed him into the house, her flip flops making desperate clattering sounds on the gravel, the screen slamming again behind her. *Papà Dios*, help me!

The boy didn't cry as she lifted him into the kitchen sink. Her mouth worked furiously as she recited the Hail Mary in her mind. (*Dios te salve, María, llena eres de gracia.*) He stared hard into her face, watched her wide-eyed. Afraid because she was afraid.

"Snoopy bit me," he said. (*El Señor es contigo.*)

"*Donde?*" But she knew.

"My wiener."

Nidia's legs tingled and her vision greyed (*Bendita tu eres entre todas las mujeres*) as she turned on the water with the only knob that worked and began washing his lower belly and thighs. (*Y bendito es el fruto de tu vientre, Jesus.*) She shouted towards the window for her closest neighbors to hear. She called each by name: Nanda! Salvador! Esmeralda! Rita! Pedro! Juriel! Yoli! Her shouts became weaker, airy, but she held out hope that someone might hear faintly, then listen more closely, then come. (*Santa Maria, Madre de Dios, ruega por nosotros, pecadores.*) But no one heard. No one answered. (*Ahora y en la hora de nuestra muerte.*) Don't look at it; I can't look at it. God, help me! (*Amen.*) She cradled the boy in her right arm and drew the thin curtain back from the window with her left. She saw nothing but the searing hot sun on the one-lane gravel road in front of her house. No one was coming.

Wrapped in a sheet, the boy laid across the backseat of Nidia's rusted green sedan for the long drive to the clinic. Blood soaked through the sheet. As Nidia carried Ricky into the whitewashed cement building with the word "clinica" hand painted in all caps over the door, one small dot of blood dripped onto the cement floor. The pudgy nurse at the reception desk attended to them immediately, a rarity. She bustled away and returned with a small young doctor who took the boy from Nidia's arms into his own. Once her hands were free, she made the sign of the cross and silently recited the Lord's Prayer. *(Padre nuestro, que estás en el cielo)* The doctor carried the boy into the nearest exam room *(santificado sea tu nombre.)* and set him gently down, *(venga tu reino)* bent over the table, and unwrapped him with his light-skinned hands. *(Hágase tu voluntad en la tierra como en el cielo.)*

"What happened?" he asked, with his head still bent over the boy. *(Danos hoy nuestro pan de cada día.)*

Nidia realized the boy hadn't made a sound since the driveway. Hadn't cried, moaned, talked, or asked questions. *(Perdona nuestras ofensas.)*

The boy answered before Nidia could. "Snoopy bit my wiener and that wasn't nice." *(Como también nosotros perdonamos a los que nos ofenden.)*

The doctor squinted at Nidia. Palms pressed together at her chest, she whispered "What will happen?" Though intent on reciting her silent prayer, her thoughts were rapid-fire, one tumbling on top of the other, vivid, jumbled: his mangled future, his parents' wrath, humiliation, legal ramifications, the faces of the orange-factory girls when they find out. Too horrible to think of. *(No nos dejes caer en tentación y líbranos del mal. Amén.)*

Nidia heard the doctor's words as if he were far away, down the dingy grey tiled corridor instead of before her. He explained that the wound was just a nick, but that any injury there bleeds like a wound to the lips or head–profusely. No more than a bit of gauze, some ointment, and rest would be necessary. The world started to come back into focus, the volume somehow raised. She felt the dread break into small pieces under her skin, liquify, seep through her pores, and evaporate into the heat.

• • •

"Why did Snoopy bite you?" Nidia gripped the steering wheel hard and concentrated on the road, looking for a roadside bar to stop at. *Just one cold Medalla.*

"I don't know."

"*Pero, papi*, why were your pants off?" She didn't take her eyes from the road to look at him.

"To play with Snoopy?" he asked.

"Why do you need your pants off to play with Snoopy?"

Silence. The tiny boy, pale and tired, was wearing a child-sized, faded hospital gown the doctor had given him for the ride home. The passenger side seatbelt was fastened over his lap and across his neck. He tilted his blond head towards the open window, ignoring her.

"Where is Snoopy's play-toy, the one he likes?" she insisted. "Did you take it?"

"I threw it in the woods."

"*Ay, Dios mio.*"

The boy stared blankly at her.

"Tell me again why you took your pants off. *Cuentame, por favor*, why did you do that?"

"To shake my wiener at Snoopy. He didn't have a toy."

Nidia pulled the car to the side of the road and stopped. She turned to look at the boy, and the two stared at each other while the car idled. Camden felt terribly far away.

The boy broke the silence, "Can I have some ice cream, Titi?"

Making Everyone Crazy

*H*ey there, Blogosphere. Let's get back to Nidia. I was hoping that if I waited a few days, I could write without being so upset, but I think it'll take more than a few days. I'm still pissed off.

Third grade started in Puerto Rico the first week of August. I left there at the end of August with a nagging reservation that Nidia might not be the right caretaker. She was going through some financial difficulties, was in between jobs, and had to move into a new house by September. She was grouchy and short with Bert and me, but seemed to be doing great with Ricky, so I overlooked it. Bert's total confidence in her helped sway me. Anyway, she loves Ricky, and it's not like we had other options.

A couple things kept bothering me, though, from the summer:

- Ricky went to PR with Nidia a few weeks before we got there. Once I arrived, I saw he had a terrible rash under his arm. I asked Titi about it and she said, oh, you know him, he's always picking at himself. Yes, he is, but did you medicate the rash? Well it would go away if he would just stop picking and scratching at it -- Ricky, stop scratching! The next day I brought him to a doctor, got a cream, and the rash went away. Of course he's going to pick and scratch if it itches!

- I had specifically asked Nidia to get a doctor's appointment for Ricky as soon as he arrived in PR, because we needed to have a local doctor know him, especially should an urgent matter arise. When I got there weeks later, she had not made any contacts with medical doctors. I made all the arrangements during my 4 week stay, and it became a part time job trying to find a specialist for him. She was getting paid to do this, but I did all the work, and spent days in doctors' offices.
- During the week while we were there, Ricky would sleep down the street at Nidia's house because she would feed him and drive him to school. We thought it would help with his transition. On Friday afternoons, she would drop him off at our house, and disappear for the weekend. She had been paid to keep him for the month. If she didn't want him for the weekends that would have been ok with me, but to presumptuously dump him on my lawn without discussing it was wierd. But I get it, she needed a break. Communication would have been nice. And certainly I wanted him around for the weekend, but we wanted him sleeping exclusively at her house to ease the transition to school. Bert kept saying that culturally, I was expecting too much. What does that even mean?

All these details had caused some of my trust in her to slide, even though Bert maintained full faith in her.

Here's why I had a crazy freak-out and yanked Ricky back home so suddenly this weekend:

It was Bert's turn to visit in October, so he went for Ricky's birthday. We did not tell Nidia Bert was coming until the day before he arrived. Two weeks earlier, I communicated by phone text, Facebook, and mail with a note and check attached, telling Nidia that Ricky wanted a bowling party for his 9th birthday. Arrange bowling, pizza, cake, and two guests, Isabel and Nicolas, who are brother and sister, (children of my husband's cousin, Evelyn). Those directions are clear, right? On Saturday, the day of his party, Nidia runs over to Evelyn's house to pick up Isabel and Nicolas, and no one is home. So she, Bert, and Ricky went to the bowling alley alone. He had no friends at his party. Of course my husband rounded up some kids in the bowling alley to sing happy birthday and eat cake, but seriously, WTH? I messaged Evelyn on Facebook (she is there 24/7), and she told me Nidia had never contacted her about any party. Now listen, Nidia can find Evelyn every day at school, because Ricky and Isabel were in the same class. Also, she could have sent invitations to school with Ricky. There were a lot of things she could have done, but didn't.

In any case, there is no excuse to send a kid to his own birthday party without having made any effort to invite his friends. I'm in a state over it. Bert doesn't understand why I'm angry over the birthday party but took the dog incident in stride. It's because I get it, it's almost impossible to keep Ricky from hurting himself sometimes. He's gotten hurt on my watch, too. But it's unacceptable for any of us to hurt him further, including his feelings. The dog nip incident–difficult to prevent. The birthday party fiasco–100% preventable.

I called Nidia to ask what happened, and she tried to play it off like, oh, well you know how it is in PR, I went to pick up the kids but Evelyn had gone out. Trying to blame it on Evelyn! When I told her I spoke with Evelyn, and she knew nothing about the party, then there was silence on the line. She tried to backpedal, saying well, I told Ricky to invite the kids. Oh, really, now eight-year-olds should be in charge of planning their own birthday parties? Come on. Seriously. That is just crazy. And that was the last straw. So I said I would have Bert bring Ricky home with him, and she says Ricky misbehaves so badly and so constantly that he's impossible and she's going crazy and she'd have his bags packed in ½ an hour. He's on the plane home with Bert right now. I can't even believe any of this happened. This didn't even last 2 months.

Stomach Ache

Hello?

[---]

I'm ok, Mom. The doctor said I'm ok and I can go home this afternoon.

[---]

I know, and I'm sorry I didn't call earlier. But I'll be out this afternoon and you can come over.

[---]

No. It was just a scare.

[---]

Yeah, a false alarm, that's all. Here's what happened. It was a totally regular morning like any other school-morning. Alex's ready and blasting his music. Hazel's running late and doing her hair for the third time. Ricky's sitting at the kitchen table, not eating his food. He was having eggs and the clam dip he likes, and we're doing what we always do. Every few minutes I turn around and say, "Ricky, eat." He briefly snaps back to being aware, and takes a bite, and then holds it there in his mouth like always because he'd drift off mentally before he finished chewing or swallowing. He'd just sit there with his mouth full of food, and then the drool would start, and his shirt would be ruined, and he'd have a fit over changing, but anyhow…my stomach was upset, but not a big deal, because it'd been upset for a few days on and off.

[---]

Yeah, it was sort of a pain like that, but different. I took that antacid for all four years of college, and they never did get to the bottom of it. But this ache wasn't the same. It was lower in my gut, down deeper. Anyway, I talked to one of my friends about it, she's a nurse, and she said it could be stress. I mean, since he's been home from PR Ricky's been doing all that stealing, and all the trouble in school. It's been constant. His friends don't like him, and all he does is roam around the house basically stealing or vandalizing.

[---]

In the house. Yeah.

[---]

I know.

[---]

So anyway, I'm standing at the kitchen counter on this regular morning, and all at once I feel this sharp pain in my left side so bad that I can't breathe, and I think I might suffocate. The air in front of me goes grey, like I might faint, and I crumple to the floor, and call down the hall for Bert, 'cause he was in the bathroom. And I'm gasping for air, and I choke out "Ricky, hey, Rick?" And I see him tip his head up to see over the table, to where I'm lying curled up in a ball on the floor. And he totally ignores me, just goes back to his eggs and takes a bite.

So I'm trying to get words out, and I feel myself losing consciousness, and I call out to Ricky again, but it's only a whisper, I say "Rick?" And he looks over at me, and by now I'm crawling on the floor towards the hallway, crying. The last thing I hear before I pass out is–

[---]

Yeah, I passed out for a minute. It hurt so bad. Anyway, the last thing I hear is, "Mom, can I have some more milk?" The kid had no concept that there was anything wrong. It was creepy as hell.

[---]

Nope, no recognition that I was in pain. If you could have seen his face.

[---]

Chilling.

[---]

I couldn't believe it either. So anyways then, evidently Hazel came out and found me, and screamed for Bert, and they drove me to the hospital. Long story short, the docs ran a bunch of tests, came up with nothing. They decided I had an "inconclusive digestive disturbance," or something like that. Which means that my stomach hurt and they don't know why.

[---]

No they don't. That's why it's called medical "practice." Just like how they told me last year my migraines were strokes, and the year before my muscle spasms were caused by a brain tumor.

[---]

You're probably right. I asked that to one of the doctors, if it could all just be stress like my friend said, and he said "absolutely."

What'd I Miss

Hey there, dear Blogosphere. Ricky and I went to see Dr. Patel today. Did I mention I hate going to Children's Specialized? We've been going there almost 5 years now, and nothing changes but the medicine. It's a useless waste of time, and it upsets Ricky and me both.

Dr. Patel asked Ricky why he had to come back from PR early.

Ricky said nonchalantly, "Because I misbehaved." (It's not fair that he thinks that, because he wasn't doing so badly. At least, no worse than usual.)

"What did you do, exactly?" asked Patel.

"I disobeyed."

"Yes, but it was more than that, wasn't it?" asked Patel.

Then Ricky cried, because it embarrasses him that people know what he does. He had to tell Patel about the stealing, destroying property, defecating on the floor, and fighting with his cousin. He was mortified.

Patel asked him, "Do you like it better here or in PR?"

"Here."

"Oh. What did you miss from here while you were in PR?"

"My toys," was the immediate response.

"Anything else?"

"The TV here is bigger."

"Anything else?" He waited while Ricky twisted his mouth to the side and looked at the ceiling. "There was nothing else or no one else you missed?"

At this point Ricky eyed me with a look that said–*Help me out, Mom. I know he's digging for something, and I don't know the right answer.* I shrugged and looked away. Ricky thought another moment, and then said with conviction "Nope! Nothing else."

I have to admit, and I know this isn't nice, but it's real, I resent devoting so much time and energy, and giving up so much of my freedom and my family's peace and normalcy, for a son I love with all my heart who doesn't even miss us when we're not around. SO not fair.

And now I have to put him back in public school. I've been doing everything to avoid it, but I'm out of options.

Black Eye Bags

Mom, you're not going to believe what happened yesterday.

[---]

No, you haven't heard it all, yet. We were out to dinner at the Carusos'. It was a long night. It was supposed to be an easy Friday night, but Ricky was having meltdowns every 15 minutes. There are no more babysitters who'll come, so we had to bring him. Or, we had to stay home, which, I feel like we're always home now. But the Caruso's have a special needs kid, so I figured they'd be ok if Ricky wasn't perfectly behaved. But I have to watch him like a hawk, because the minute I don't he's wandering where he doesn't belong, like upstairs in people's bedrooms or in the basement.

[---]

So it wasn't fun at all. I could barely carry on a conversation because I had to tail Ricky, or else I had to hold him with me by his wrist while he shouted and flailed around. It was awful. When we left, I was in my heels and carrying a little patent leather wristlet, you know the cute black one from Coach? So I walked out first, then Alex and Hazel. Bert was still in the house, I thought, with Ricky. So out of nowhere Ricky comes out of the door like a shot and runs past me into the driveway and into the snow. The Caruso house is on top of a hill, so he makes a bee-line for the driveway and starts squealing that he's going to slide in the snow. The driveway ends onto a relatively quiet street, but down the street I see headlights. The snow is thick. If he slides down the driveway he will end up in the street, and he probably won't realize that he has to get up and get out of the way of the car.

[---]

This is the exact scenario that the doctor had used a couple years ago to explain the disconnect between what he knows and how to put that knowledge into action. He said an FAS kid can see a car coming, tell you he sees it, all the while plummeting towards the road on a sled on a crash course with the car. There is no connection between the car he sees, his travelling towards the road, and realizing that he could get hit.

[---]

Knowing this, and mind you this is all going on in my head in a matter of nanoseconds, I jump towards him, teetering on my new heels that I got for Christmas, the maroon leather ones, I love them, and I lunge for him with both hands, like I'm practically horizontal, knowing that I'll probably fall, chest first, onto the driveway and into the snow, if I'm going to have a chance to catch him before he hurls himself sliding down the driveway. So I'm flying through the air, but remember the wristlet?

[---]

Mara Kendahl

Both my hands just miss him, but somehow the wristlet swings and catches him right on the side of his face between his temple and his eye before I end up face first on the driveway.

[---]

Yes, we're both ok. But you know how he does, he lets out a shriek and crumples to the ground, his default reaction whenever he's angry that you've seen a zillion times. I think it shocked him more than hurt him, though, because it takes a lot to hurt him. So anyway, great that I stopped him from throwing himself down the hill, but certainly not the way I wanted to. I scooped him up, cooed and petted, and we drove home with him mad as all hell in my lap. He got a little bruise by his eye, but no damage, no harm done. Poor kid, I felt so bad. As if he doesn't have enough trouble, now he has to get whacked in the eye.

False

———Original Message———

From: Margot
To: Teacher, Teacher's Aide
Cc: Principal, School Psychologist
Subject: Ricky

Dear Teacher and Teacher's Aide,

This letter is in answer to your complaints to the authorities (who have dismissed your claims):

1) That I purposefully hit Ricky with my handbag and bruised his eye: **False**.

Ricky got hit in the eye with my wristlet when he was running down a snowy driveway towards the street on the night of Sunday, January 23rd. As I grabbed for him, my purse swung from my wrist and hit him above his left eye. There was a small bruise above his eye on Monday, January 24th. (I would hope that in the future, if you truly believe a child to be in danger from abusive parents, you would not wait an entire week to call the authorities.) Also, between Monday, January 24, and Monday, January 31 (the day of your call), Ricky was seen by his specialist at Children's Specialized Hospital and his Trinitas Hospital DYFS caseworker.

You are aware that Ricky is permanently developmentally disabled. I have provided all paperwork to the school system. He has social awareness difficulties, as well as issues with stealing and lying. He does not fully understand abstract concepts such as intentions of others or ownership. You should have brought your concerns to me or the school psychologist for her consideration before you take the word of a child who cannot understand. Over the past month I have been in contact weekly with the school psychologist as well as occasionally with the superintendent, explaining that my son is becoming increasingly mentally confused and unstable, and asking for assistance. I received the opposite.

2) That because Ricky is skinny and his ribs show, I must be withholding food from him as punishment: **False**.

Besides feeding him 3 meals, snacks, and supplements daily, I have 7+ years of documentation showing my complaints to his doctors and specialists that Ricky has failed to thrive. His growth and weight gain have always been monitored, due to his small size and poor weight gain. Ricky has been put on prescriptions that cause obesity, and has not gained any weight while on these medications. No matter how much he is fed or what supplements he takes, he continues to be skinny. Monday, January 24, my husband and I were again asking his doctor at Children's Specialized Hospital what we could do about his size. We were told "nothing". That is what most children with his diagnosis look like: frail, skinny, small stature. We have worked hard with this small skinny boy, to do the best with what he has. Because of our efforts, expenses, and nurturing, he is an excellent athlete despite his challenges. He was chosen for the "A Team" in baseball, he is an accomplished swimmer, diver, and gymnast and, as you know, placed 3rd in the town wide hoop shoot. We taught him how to juggle for coordination, and he is an expert with both hands. Regarding food, we overfeed him, arguing daily over how much food he has to finish. We cater to his likes and introduce new foods constantly in hopes that he will eat more. Because of this, he has an excellent palate, and his favorite foods include asparagus, raspberries, and clams.

3) That Ricky dresses in thrift store clothing while the rest of the family sports new clothing: **False**.

Ricky has obsessions as well as sensory issues. We have struggled for years to dress Ricky appropriately, which has caused too many morning ordeals with tears and breakdowns before breakfast. He has preferences for old clothes and his brother's hand-me-downs. He has a dresser full of new clothing (well documented and observed by the Behavior Assistant that Trinitas Hospital sends to the house weekly). He chooses not to wear these clothes. When forced to wear them, he will cut them, tear them, and sometimes urinate on them. I don't choose to fight this battle. As long as Ricky is dressed warmly enough, I allow him to wear what makes him happy.

4) That we "left" Ricky in Puerto Rico: **False**.

We spent 3 years planning his possible relocation to Puerto Rico. He is less mentally confused, and has fewer serious behavior issues when he is in a rural setting and a climate that allows ample outdoor play. We arranged this plan with the help of his doctor, his therapist, and the school system in Puerto Rico. We tested the plan slowly, letting him live with his aunt for summers only. I was present for all the special education meetings in Puerto Rico, as well as his first day and first month of school. He had a doctor monitoring his medication, a social worker handling his case, and special education services in place in PR before I returned to NJ. Also, because Ricky has symptoms of Attachment Disorder, he was quite happy to stay in his aunt's home. He returned in October because I felt his aunt was having difficulty liking him after he repeatedly stole from her and disobeyed her. My husband flew down and brought Ricky home.

In sum, your accusations were all false, knee-jerk reactions to the first mark you have ever seen on my child. You've been harboring a poor opinion of me based on his appearance and my family's background. When you saw his bruise, you allowed your personal prejudices regarding his weight, his clothing, and his status as an adopted child to cloud your judgment. You gossiped about his physical appearance, his adoption, and your assumptions about us to others (yes, things get back to me!).

You made assumptions and judgments regarding my family's decision to seek a more tranquil setting for him in PR. Bottom line: You placed further stress on a family and children that are already struggling. You did not partner with his family in his care. You made rash decisions based on your own prejudices. Therefore, to keep Ricky and the rest of my family safe from the harm judgmental people like yourselves can cause, I plan to remove Ricky from school in the near future.

Margot

PS. Heads up: Ricky wanted to know why the strangers came on Monday night to embarrass him by making him remove his shirt and pull down his pants. I told him the truth. That his teachers sent them. That you said I hit him, don't feed him enough, or buy him new clothes. He expressed disappointment in both of you for lying and may confront you. Please be adult enough not to worry about defending yourselves, but think of this little boy's feelings and best interest when answering. "I'm sorry, I made a mistake" might work for him.

Hazel's Concert

There's black ladies in the driveway in black lady dresses walking slow with big boobs. My dress is prettier. So nervous! Everyone will hear me sing, and see me! I should put a different clip in my hair. Momma likes this one but I liked the other one with the yellow sparkles. Maybe I'll stand next to Billy. I love the winter concert so much! Last year's winter concert I had to stand by Katie on one side and Jarrod on the other and Jarrod doesn't even sing and then maybe everyone can hear me more. Yellow sparkles are nice with this dress. Pretty pink dress, so happy! It twirls when I twirl and it's like a princess dress.

Momma's in the front door calling to the ladies, telling them they're late. A day late. Why are they here tonight? They say they aren't late, so she let them in. Why is she letting them IN?! It's not a day for visitors we have to do my hair!! Now they're at the kitchen table and Momma's making tea and talking with her annoyed face at the ladies. They're calling for

Ricky. Everyone always calls for Ricky. Maybe I can wear some makeup and Momma won't notice.

Now Ricky's crying. Again. He's stomping to his room and slamming the door. He's so loud. Always a problem with Ricky. Throwing things in Ricky's room.

"Momma, do my hair."

She gave me the look. I better get out of here but WHO is going to do my hair? I can. I'll just brush it a little bit like, just to the side a little, and maybe some gel, and then a pin and my clip. I can get some more clips, and the yellow one. One bobby pin on the side, nice, holds my hair back pretty like a movie star. Now another on top of it so it won't come out. Now some hair spray that Momma keeps in her room but she never uses it. Why doesn't Momma ever do her hair? It's so short like a boy, but she used to wear it long and pretty when I was a baby. I don't remember too much but I like to look at all the pictures. I'm going to make my hair look like Momma's used to. Maybe some more hairspray. Momma can never be a princess with short hair. Some pink lipstick, just a little, and I look so pretty.

Momma's calling my name loud, my real name not Sugar. I better run. She looks unhappy. She said let's go in her rushed voice, but then she sees me and she looks more unhappy, like maybe I should have worn the other hair clip.

She rushes me in the bathroom and tries to brush my hair but OUCH, Mom, stop! Owwwww! She is fussing and pulling and the clips won't come out and she rubbed my face SO HARD to get the lipstick off and it looked to nice. And she's in a hurry. I want to cry but I won't because maybe everyone at the concert will be able to tell I was crying if I cry.

"Momma, are we late?" What if I don't get there on time? I'll die.

"Yes." And she put my hair in a ponytail, and it's sticking up and out all over the place and we're late and I don't look nice and everyone's going to see me. She took Ricky out of his room and she has to hold him by his arm because he's kicking and screaming again like he likes to do and I look terrible and now I'm crying, too, and my face is wet and my nose is running, because the black ladies didn't have to come over tonight and ruin everything. I hate the stupid winter concert!

More Eye Bags

Hi Mom, all good?
[---]
C'mon, you know it's never all good here.
[---]
OK, remember I told you about how my purse caught Ricky in the eye that night at the Carusos'?
[---]
No, it's not over, Mom, nothing's ever over. A couple days later in school, the helper teacher, that little teenager in her first job, unqualified, hired only because her grandmother works at the high school for like ever, looked at me sideways when I showed up to pick Ricky up after school. Later that night while I was helping Hazel get ready for the winter concert, doing her hair and listening to her little hopes and fears about the concert, and about her dress, and her songs, and her hair, two ladies from DYFS showed up at the door asking about why Ricky had a black eye.
[---]

Mara Kendahl

I kid you not. They show up in the driveway, calling out and waving like we're old friends. I told them they were a day late, because remember how over the weekend Ricky was cutting himself and sneaking out of the house at night? I was so exhausted staying up, barely sleeping, to make sure that he was asleep before I could sleep, and then waking up with every tiny sound because I'm afraid he's hurting himself or leaving the house, so I called the DYFS help line for when a kid is out of control supposedly they are supposed to come to your house and help or take him to the hospital overnight for observation. I needed them to take him for observation because if I can't get any sleep, I'm going to end up in the hospital again. I need some relief, seriously, what'll it be next? So when I called them they asked what Ricky was doing, and I said he was awake in his room. They asked if he was out of control. I said no, I just told you he's awake in his room, just sitting in his bed. But if I go to sleep he will injure himself or leave the house. Is he injuring himself now, they asked me. I told them no, so they said if he's not in immediate danger right now, they won't come. So I said does he need to hurt himself or leave the house first? They said he had to be uncontrollable. But if I go to sleep, then who is controlling him. They said it doesn't work like that. So I argued some more, then cried, but they still said they wouldn't come. They said even if I brought him to the hospital, they'd release him right back to me. So facetiously I said what if I tie him up to keep him safe while I sleep? That's illegal, they said. The logic...

[---]

So when I told them they were a day late, they didn't know what I was talking about. I said aren't you here to check up on

Ricky. Yes, they said. I called you for help yesterday, I said, why are you here now? I don't need you now. Well, they said, we're not here because YOU called. So I knew there was gonna be a problem and I knew right away it was that teenage whore helper teacher who emails Ricky on the weekends and has him look at her slutty little music videos of her online in a mini skirt shaking her skinny ass. Pathetic. So in they come and I seat them all nice at the kitchen table and start making them some tea, and they called Ricky and took off his shirt and made him pull his pants down and his underwear.

[---]

Yeah, right in the kitchen in front of these two strangers, he was so mad. He looked at me with his little face like asking do I have to? But I don't think I could have said no, could I? Then they might have taken him and he'd be even madder and I would be in that nightmare snag of having to deal with the courts to get him back. Better to just cooperate and get it over with quick.

[---]

Of course he was mortified. His little face was red and he pulled his pants up so hard and fast and mad almost to his little neck and stormed out of the kitchen crying. Then I had to make nice and explain the whole episode to the ladies, and they were nice, but I couldn't rush them out. They were taking their sweet time. But I said we had to go to a concert and perhaps they'd like to come back tomorrow. Finally they left, saying no need to come back, that clearly it was a misunderstanding. Then I still had to figure out Hazel, you know this was her big night. She's been practicing those songs and trying on every dress in her closet for weeks. So while I was talking to the ladies she had made a mess of herself and I had to fix her and bring Ricky squalling and raging, and we were already running late which made Hazel wild. We were all crying by the time we got in the car. It was a disaster.

Fairy Tale Part 6: Miracle

Luckily, on the open prairie in the Wild West there was a ranch for kids where Ricky was invited to live, learn discipline, and grow up healthy and happy. But even the Wild West couldn't tame him. He was destined for jail, or worse! His new mommy feared she couldn't keep him safe and healthy. She had to find a mommy who could, before it was too late…

Why

Hey Blogosphere, how's everything? Me? Oh, awful, thanks for asking. I feel so discouraged. Today was a mess. Nothing out of the ordinary, though. Sometimes I ask myself how we all got into this mess. You've heard the old saying "it seemed like a good idea at the time." Well, it really did.

I remember, in the wake of 9/11, when Americans were pulling together, or at least we folks in NY/NJ were, it seemed that there were so many opportunities, small ones, to make the world a better place. Volunteer, donate money, donate blood, be part of the solution. At this same time, in my little household, we were thinking about whether we should go for a third pregnancy or not. I was of the opinion that three children would be a good number. I grew up in a household with three kids. Bert grew up in a household with 10 kids. We were leaning towards going for it.

But I had always had adoption in the back of my mind. Maybe because I'm an adopted kid. Or maybe it was because of that story about the kid who walked along the beach in the morning, where thousands of starfish had washed up on the shore. Do you know that story? The kid picks up one starfish at a time, and tosses it back into the ocean. An adult comes by asks him why he's bothering to throw them back in, one by one, when there are thousands. He can't possibly hope to make a difference. The boy picks up one starfish and replies, " I know I can't make a difference, but to this one…" and here he throws the starfish back into the waves, "I have just made all the difference in the world." I know it's corny, but it's also true.

Anyway, the applications for adoption were a nightmare. I almost quit before I started. You'd have to be desperate, I thought. But before paperwork, we had to decide where to adopt from and which agency to use.

I investigated which agency to use for over a month. (So many options, so confusing!) I started with my local DYFS office in NJ. I called and asked to speak to someone about adoption. I was transferred to a woman with no personality, who did not seem happy to answer the phone. I told her my husband and I were interested in exploring adoption. After inquiring about our residence, employment, income, and backgrounds, she said "you don't qualify." Um, why? We both work, we have two children, live in our own home in the suburbs, have excellent income and recommendations from our bosses and pastors, what is disqualifying us? She said you can't have a White baby, because your husband is Hispanic. Therefore, you can't offer a White household, so you don't qualify. OMG. First of all, I never asked for a White baby, but OK, so how about a Hispanic baby? Same response, because I am White, we can't offer a Hispanic household to the child, so we don't qualify. Is this a joke? So I said I know the system has many African-American children waiting for homes. We are willing. Nope, you don't qualify. C'mon. So then she says, "Buuuuut," and goes on to say if you'd like a handicapped child, you can take your pick. Wait, I say, do you mean to tell me that White children have the right to a White household, Hispanic children have the right to a Hispanic Household, and Black children have the right to a Black Household, but disabled children have no such rights as you have just explained them? She said she could see we were not the type of family she could work with, and hung up. (Years later, I told this story to my case worker from Trinitas Hospital who works closely with DYFS. She said she wasn't surprised, because there is so much turnover in DYFS and the workers are barely trained and often unsupervised.)

Fine. American semi-open adoptions sort of freak me out anyway. I had had a lingering uneasiness as a child that some strangers could one day show up and claim rights to me. I was just as happy avoiding open adoption. I didn't want anyone interfering with my family. So where to go? Romania seemed to be "closed." China did not feel like a good option. First, I was certain I wanted a boy, and I had been told boys were much harder to place than girls. I wonder why that is? Also, we were already a "minority" family in a White town. Adding a third race was certainly going to single us out as "that" family.

It turns out that Russia, in 2001 when I began to investigate, was listed as having over 600,000 children in its orphanages.

What an astronomical number! I called a number of local agencies. They were abrupt on the phone, mean, rude. Once I got Joseph from Children's Home on the phone, I knew I could work with him. He spent time explaining the process. He wasn't being nosy, asking for money upfront, or inquiring about my walk with Christ. He was responsive, knowledgeable, and willing to answer my questions. He helped me get all my paperwork and my homestudy in order, and billed me after his work was done and not before.

Then, after all the paperwork was done, we got a referral. (Oh, the homestudy and paperwork. They took months. And money.) Then, abruptly, I couldn't contact Joseph. A few days passed, and he called me to explain that his agency had been closed down by the state of NJ, and my paperwork had been confiscated and locked in a vault in Cherry Hill, NJ. Money gone, work gone, paperwork gone, referral cancelled.

Clearly, they didn't know me. I called the head of NJ Social Services (twice a day for two and a half weeks) and the Star Ledger (and my lawyer, always my lawyer!) to get my paperwork back. Then, randomly, some agency from Utah, Focus on Children, steps in to take on the rest of my case and see it to completion. Some work that had been paid for had to be redone. (All adoption documents for the Russian government expire after three months.) Tanya from Focus on Children said she didn't like working with Amrex, an evil Russian adoption agency that serves as a middle-man, but that the Russian government gave her no choice. She was not as easy to work with as Joseph, but she was a nice woman, if a little short on personality.

So finally, after months, (which meant if we wanted to continue we had to redo all our paperwork) we got another "referral." It was a video of a red-haired boy, about 2 years old, standing next to a table, holding it for balance. The video lasted about 2 minutes. The child never let go of the table, though there were Russian voices off-camera coaxing him. I brought this video to my children's pediatrician, who said, "That child is not right. I don't believe he can walk." I told the agency I refused.

Weeks later, we were sent another "referral." The child was hearty and smiling. The pediatrician had nothing negative to say. OK, here we go. I bought a ticket to Khabarovsk, Far East Region, Russia. I went alone, and Bert stayed home with the kids, Alex 4 and Hazel 2. The rest is history.

Interestingly, Joyce at the ranch told me last week that Focus on Children got shut down a couple years after our case. When I said I had used Focus, she said, "Oh, them. They thought they were so smart." I didn't want to ask what she meant, so I googled it later. Focus was tricking families somewhere in the South Pacific into giving up their babies, and they got caught. Nasty stuff.

The rest, well, after getting royally jerked around, we went for our second trip, got Ricky home, and that's when all hell broke loose. And it's been hell ever since. And it's hell every day. And it's hell right this minute. Especially for Ricky. At this point, Bert and I are considering some drastic measures to save the family. Not sure I'm ready to talk about it yet. Oops, but I already mentioned Joyce.

A Wild West Inquiry

Dear Sir or Ma'am,

I am writing to inquire about your school for kids with FAS on the Ranch for Kids in Montana. I have read all the material on your website, ranchforkids.org. Is your facility only for children whose families are considering adoption disruption? I would not like to disrupt my adoption, but I cannot find a suitable school program for my son. Also, my family is coming undone around my son's disruptive behavior. Your facility seems ideal. In case you have no openings, do you know of any other schools anywhere in the United States that specialize in FAS? I can find many for ADHD, Autism, and Asperger's, but none that seem to understand the special needs of FAS kids as you do.
    Thanks in advance for your kind attention.

Best regards,
Margot

Paradigm

Hello?
[---]
I'm glad you're home. Mom, this ranch might be the answer. I spoke to the director this morning, Joyce, she seems to get the big picture. She said social services knows what to do with dysfunctional children in dysfunctional families. They have no idea what to do with dysfunctional children in normal households. It is against their paradigm, she said. Can you believe that? I wish I said that myself.
[---]
It's a therapeutic boarding school. She said they rehabilitate kids who've set fires, killed pets, molested siblings, vandalized and stolen, and all sorts of other crazy stuff. It seems like Ricky might be sort of normal on the ranch. Not like I want him with a bunch of crazies, but they really have a handle on these kids. They do better after they've been there a while. They live pretty simply and peacefully from what I gather.
[---]

I don't like sending him, either, but we're falling apart over here. I've gotta do something. They know what to do on the ranch, how to help, and then after he's learned to regulate himself, he can come home!

[---]

No, I guess I don't. But I think it's in his best interest to get out of this environment a while. He does so well in the open air, with a set schedule, and animals like in PR. We can't offer any of that here.

[---]

I'm afraid he's about to get himself taken by DYFS and thrown into foster care because of this crazy talk he's been tossing around at school. Yesterday he told a girl that he has a penis collection at home. What that's about, I don't know, but I'm expecting another visit from DYFS any minute. You know they don't take into account that he's mentally disabled and on medication. If he says it, they believe it, and none of us needs that.

[---]

I have no idea what a penis collection is.

[---]

I know. Everything is crazy.

[---]

Maybe it is. And the rest of us need some normal, even if it's just for a couple of months. I figure we can only afford to keep him there a couple of months anyway; it costs a fortune. But it's better than nothing. Alex and Hazel are starting to unravel. Ricky seems agitated and confused more than usual lately. I have no idea how to make this better.

[---]

No, I don't think so. But I'm barely holding it together around here anymore, and frankly, I don't know how to keep him safe. I haven't slept in weeks because he keeps getting up at night and sneaking around. Sometimes he lets himself out of the house.

[---]

I called. I was hoping they might hospitalize him just one night so I could get some sleep, but they said they'll only come out if he's uncontrollable. If he's docile, they release him back to me. I'm considering hospitalizing myself just to get some sleep.

[---]

I'm heartbroken, too, for all of us, but something's gotta give. I don't know what else to do.

Recurring Drama

Margot: Can we talk about this? The ranch?

Bert: Ugh…

Margot: We can't put if off forever.

Bert: I don't like it.

Margot: There's only an opening *now*. If we don't take it, someone else will. The waiting list can be years.

Bert: I'm against any idea that sends him away from family.

Margot: He went to PR and loved it.

Bert: PR is different. That's not sending him away. He's in his own neighborhood with his own family. Montana is completely different. I don't like it.

Margot: I don't like it either, but I'm afraid of what will happen if we don't send him. DYFS is on our backs now, and he's been getting stranger and stranger. The types of conversations he's having at school are enough for them to start taking kids first and asking questions later. It happens to families with disabled kids. The kid says some nonsense at school, and DYFS shows up at the door later. They have to investigate. They can take him first and sort it out later. I'm not willing to risk that. Honestly, do you think Ricky'll be safe even for a day in foster care? He'll hurt himself or someone else. No one would be prepared for him.

Bert: Over my dead body anyone's going to take him. They can't do that.

Margot: Of course they can. It's what they do. Be realistic.

Bert: DYFS or no, we're not going to send a kid away. None of this is his fault.

Margot: Well, we agree on something, then. You're right, it's not his or anyone's fault. But we need to find a solution right now that's going to work for everyone. Especially Ricky. He's the one at the most risk here. We can't just keep going, waiting for disaster.

Bert: Are we really going to be those people who send their kid away when the going gets tough?

Margot: It's not about sending him away. It's about giving him a chance. It's about keeping him safe. I'm afraid for him. I don't think he's going to have those options. He's going to end up institutionalized. If we handle it now, we still have a say. If we wait, it might be the government, or legal, or medical people making the decision for us. Also, I'm starting to be worried for Hazel. It's enough that she's missing her front tooth. But the whole thing with his cousin over the summer,...it's only a matter of time. I've already put locks on everyone's bedroom door, but that's not even safe either. What if there's a fire? How will they get out? And you know he can't be left alone ever. Ever.

Bert: What is the ranch supposed to accomplish? No one else ever accomplished anything, and now these magic ranch people think they can make a difference?

Margot: It's a therapeutic group home. The woman who runs it says that the kids get up and do chores, they care for the animals, they go to school on site, and they have a whole system of discipline and earning privileges that really works. It doesn't work quickly, it can take months, but in a group environment they all get on board sooner or later she says. She said she wanted to be upfront with me and not try to convince me that this is any type of cure. Take him off the ranch, and he goes back to his old behaviors. But on the ranch, there's a good chance that he can learn how to regulate himself in this group and get through school. It'll give him a chance to be successful for once. Isn't that reason enough? Imagine it, the fresh air, the horses and animals, the simplicity. Isn't it sad to see him failing all the time? This could be his chance to feel great about himself, finally. Doesn't he deserve that?

Bert: So we keep him there until he gets better and then we bring him back. You said they think they need a few months?

Margot: That's not what I said.

Bert: And how do we explain this to him and the kids?

Margot: The same way we explained going to school in PR. A fun opportunity.

Bert: What about everyone else?

Margot: Everyone else can go to hell for all I care.

Bert: Yeah, but you know it's not like that.

Margot: I know.

Bert: How much is this going to set us back? Will insurance cover any of it?

Margot: A lot, and no. But here's the thing, we started a college fund for him when he was little, and there's not much in it, but what there is, we can spend. It doesn't look like college is going to be an option.

Bert: I don't know.

Margot: To me, this doesn't feel like sending a kid away, even though I know that everyone else is going to see it that way. I don't care how everyone else sees it. Let's put your feelings and my feelings aside and worry about what's best for him. Let's put everything aside and worry about what's best for only him, short term and long term.

Bert: But that's not how things work.

Margot: Says who? Who makes the rules? We need to do what's right, not what everyone else thinks is acceptable. I already said it, and I mean it, to hell with everyone else. You know he doesn't miss us when we're gone. If I thought he'd miss us and feel lonely, it would be a different story. As long as he has his toys and the TV programs he likes, he's not going to care that we're not around. We're going to miss him, but he's not going to miss us. No use feeling sorry for something that isn't happening. Other nine-year-olds might feel terrible. But not him, and you know it.

Bert: I feel ashamed to even think about sending my son away.

Margot: Get over yourself. You're worried about people and appearances. I would feel ashamed *not* to send him when I know that it would be the best thing for him. Maybe not the best thing for you and your feelings, maybe not the best thing for me, I'll be talked about in this town forever, but I know it's the best thing for him. How can we withhold this opportunity for him to be successful and live in peace and finally feel good about himself? Just because it's inconvenient for us? Embarrassing for us? What about him?

Bert: What kind of parents send their children away?

Margot: Should we go down to the church and talk to a minister about it?

Bert: No.

Intercession

Dear Lord,

You are the ruler of all things in heaven and earth, all creatures and creations bow to Your power. I'm eternally grateful for the gifts and blessings given because of Your abundant love for me, even though I'm a sinner. Thank You, Lord, for hearing me and for being ready to listen to all of my earthly problems when I come to You. Only You provide all things good, Lord, and no other power can come before You. You are so great, and all powerful, and I thank you for your presence in my life, Father.

Lord, I'm coming to you on my knees with a prayer of intercession for Margot, a mother who's hurting. As her pastor, I ask that you hear my prayer on her behalf. Please give her wisdom, nourish her budding faith, and hold her in the palm of Your hand through this darkness. Let her feel your strength, your majesty, and your love. Overwhelm her, Lord, with the power and presence of Your Holy Spirit.

You know her problems, God, and her family's pain. I pray you help her make the best decision, the one that's right in Your eyes. Lead her from fear to trust. Be a lamp to her feet and a light to her path. Provide the courage and comfort that only You can. She needs Your help now, O God; please hear her prayer.

All power and glory to You, Lord. Nothing is beyond your reach; nothing is impossible, Father God. You can move mountains. You've taught us that all who call on You in faith will be heard and will receive what they have asked.

Thank You, Almighty God, for Your greatness and Your love, for hearing my prayer, and for Your promise of salvation and eternal life. All this I pray in the Holy Name of Jesus.

Amen.

Welcome to the Ranch

Hi Margot,

I thought I would give you a quick update on Ricky. He has been pretty quiet. I think he is "sizing us up." The first day he was here he stole my phone and we had a visitor who came from the airport with him, and he stole her Kindle. I found it in his bag. He didn't have much to say about it. He has been cooperative with chores thus far, but did voice his displeasure to the other kids about having to do them. He has been a bit resistant eating his food, but eventually does eat it. I am sure as he gets more comfortable we will see more behaviors.

If I can answer any questions for you, please feel free to call me anytime on my cell.

Angie

Keep It Clean

——— Original Message ———

From: Margot
To: Dr. Patel
Subject: RE: update

Dear Dr. Patel,

Regarding your request to keep you in the loop regarding Ricky's progress at the Ranch, I'm writing to inform you that it is too early to expect any progress, he's only been there 2 weeks, but I'll report nonetheless.

Ricky's counselor, Angela, reports that he's been making himself unpleasant to others with inappropriate conversations and a contradictory attitude. He stole a couple items the first weekend he was there, including a cell phone and a Kindle. He pooped his bed on Friday night and had to clean it himself. Evidently, he made quite a scene raging over cleaning it.

Mara Kendahl

He pooped his bed again on Saturday night, and again had to clean it himself, and had another full blown raging tantrum to rival the first one. I think he poops to show his displeasure. When he was angry with his aunt over the summer he pooped in her house a few times. This is the first time he's had to wash it himself. Honestly, I can't imagine how they got him to clean it. Angela said that other kids have done this, evidently it's not uncommon, and they usually learn after a few times of cleaning it and washing the sheets by hand that they don't want to continue the behavior. I hope this will be the case with Ricky, too. He is learning the hard way, as usual. I'm glad the Ranch staff are so calm, consistent, and firm with him. I think eventually he will respond well in that type of environment.

On a positive note, Ricky (according to Ricky) is excelling in school and has been moved up to 4th grade reading, as a 3rd grader! Yeay! He is an excellent reader, no doubt about that. Also, he says he plays basketball most days with a sixth grader. Ricky can compete in hoops with anyone.

Please feel free to call or email me with further questions. Thank you, again, for agreeing to prescribe Ricky's medication until we can find an arrangement in Montana.

Best regards,
Margot

Ask

Anonymous note found by an assistant to the Reverend Mary Julia Jett among the tithes and offerings after Sunday's 11:00 AM Choral Eucharist Service at the Cathedral Church of Saint John the Divine, 1047 Amsterdam Avenue at 112th Street, Upper West Side, New York City.

Dear Jesus,

I've been referred to you by my pastor, who said you would hear my request even though we don't know each other well. Following please find a list of things I'm sure my son needs, and I'm hoping you can provide, because clearly I cannot.

1. Two loving, experienced parents with good morals and solid faith
2. Parents with no other children (I know this is not plausible given item #1, but I was told to ask for everything and let you handle the details.)

Mara Kendahl

---

3. Family life that revolves around structure and discipline
4. A strict and involved father
5. A mother with experience in health care, teaching, and special education
6. Outdoor play possibilities year round in a secure area
7. Animals to care for
8. A calmer, slower environment than the NY metropolitan area
9. Family, friends, and peers with working class expectations
10. Opportunities to shine and succeed

Please reply at your earliest convenience. Note that anything you can do to expedite delivery would be greatly appreciated. Thank you sincerely and in advance for your kind attention to this matter. In hopes of an outcome that is mutually agreeable, I am

Very truly yours,

(I'd sign, but my pastor said you'll know already.)

And Ye Shall Receive

Dear Margot,

Hi, my name is Cindi from Wasatch Adoptions in Washington State. Joyce at the Ranch for Kids referred me to you. I know we don't know each other, but she said I should discuss an opportunity with you. Please see the description below of a family I represent that Joyce and I think you should meet:

Bob and Carol are good Christian parents hoping to adopt a special needs child. Bob grew up on a ranch in Kentucky, and Carol on a farm in Ohio. They've raised their three children to adulthood (their boy, now 24, is special needs) and feel called to start a new family. They are still young, mid- 40's, and hope to be a blessing to another special needs boy. Both Bob and Carol are enlisted in the U.S. Army, and they're stationed on a military base in Germany, where they live in family-style housing with their 2 dogs. Bob specializes in mechanics and coaches in the kids' baseball league. Carol is a school nurse and kindergarten teacher.

Mara Kendahl

This past Monday, Bob and Carol suffered a disappointment. They were supposed to have taken custody of a little boy, a 10-year-old Russian adoptee who's been living on the Ranch for over a year, but their legal case fell apart abruptly on Sunday evening when the custodial parents unexpectedly decided not to go through with the transfer we've all been working on for so long. They are devastated. Joyce suggested we set up a meeting to see you. These people have ready arms and big hearts. Will you please consider meeting with us?

I look forward to a conversation with you, even if you are not ready to make any commitments at this time.

God bless you,
Cindi

• • •

Sources

Bonnie Miller Rubin | Chicago Tribune. "The Final Stop for Disruptive Adoptees." *Los Angeles Times*. Los Angeles Times, 20 Jan. 2008. Web. 23 Apr. 2017.

Burleigh, Nina. "A Dad's Adoption Nightmare – Vol. 71 No. 24." *PEOPLE.com*. Time Inc, 22 June 2009. Web. 23 Apr. 2017.

Johnson, Kirk. "Russian Adoptees Get a Respite on the Range." *The New York Times*. The New York Times, 26 Apr. 2010. Web. 23 Apr. 2017.

Pearson, Michael. "Adoption Services Firm Investigated Over Missing Funds." *The Atlanta Journal-Constitution* 03 Oct. 2006: Print.

Tribolet, Beth, Teri Whitcraft, Scott Michels, Abc News Law, and Justice Unit. "Four Sentenced in Scheme to 'Adopt' Samoan Kids." *ABC News*. ABC News Network, 26 Feb. 2009. Web. 23 Apr. 2017.

Tolman, Brett L. "Fact Sheet on Focus On Children Adoption Fraud Case." *U.S. Department of State*. District of Utah, 1 Mar. 2007. Web. 23 Apr. 2017.

www.ingramcontent.com/pod-product-compliance
Lightning Source LLC
LaVergne TN
LVHW011153080426
835508LV00007B/380